TABLE OF CONTENTS

IS THIS BOOK FOR YOU

WHO STOLE MY COPYRIGHTS?

GET YOUR PAPER RIGHT

GETTING BOOK DISTRIBUTION

BRANDING, PROMOTIONS, PUBLICITY

TEN WAYS TO MAKE MONEY FROM YOUR BOOK

HOW TO SELF

PUBLISH

FOR

PROFIT

Resources for:
Authors, Writers, Book Publishers

by
JAWAR

1

Copyright 2007 JAWAR
ISBN 10 DIGIT: 0-9759380-5-3
ISBN 13 DIGIT: 978-0-9759380-5-8
Library of Congress Control Number: 2006940501

by JaWar

FIRST EDITION

Published by

Music Industry Connection, LLC
P.O. Box 52682, Atlanta, GA 30355, USA
800-963-0949, 678-887-4656
www.gojawar.com, makemoneyselfpublishing.com

The information provided in this book is intended only as a resource guide for aspiring artist, producers, engineers and managers in the music industry. Remember to always verify the company and contact names found in this book before submitting material. There are a number of resources needed to achieve success as a self-publisher that are not contained in this book. The author and publisher have attempted to verify the accuracy of the resources in this book; however, the information provided is subject to change. The author and publisher disclaim all responsibility for any loss or damages.

The goal of the author is to provide a how to resource tool, reference guide and directory for writers, authors and self-publishers.

How to Self-Publish for Profit is designed to give writers, authors and self-publishers practical steps and tips for achieving their goals and realizing their success.

Cover Design by Ashil for Design Apart 404-351-4312
Edited by Seneferu Aset

WHAT YOU DIDN'T KNOW TO ASK ABOUT SELF-PUBLISHING?

WHAT YOU NEED TO KNOW ABOUT SELF-PUBLISHING?

IS THIS BOOK FOR YOU?

As an aspiring author, are you seeking a royalty rate of 3% to 11% off the retail-selling price per unit on the books you wrote? Are you seeking to give total editing control to someone who is not familiar with your writing style, personality or vision for your book? Are you seeking to give up ownership of your intellectual property i.e. copyrights that may generate hundreds of thousands if not millions of dollars over the life of the copyright (the life of the copyright being the life of the creator/writer/author (you) plus seventy some odd years)?

After taking months (if not years) of writing, you must now promote your manuscript to a group of people who may not be familiar with your writing style or inspired by your work. They may not have a clue on how to promote your book to your target market. Your writing future may be left in the hands of complete strangers; people who are many miles and moons from where you live or where your target market frequents. This is but a glimpse into your future as an aspiring author.

Many writers seek the traditional publishing route for a number of reasons, primarily due to fear or ignorance. Fear that they will not succeed; fear that they don't have enough start up capital; fear that they will do something wrong or "mess up" something; fear of talking to people; fear of taking control of their own destiny; fear of not being accepted; fear of being a trail blazer and a host of other fears that make me sick... these fears often stop people from doing something different.

Because of the lack of proper information, education, guidance, resources and experience, we are often ignorant on how to do something. The continued lack of proper information prevents us from knowing about book publishing. The lack of proper information does not grant us the ability to look at different vantage points as it relates to having a book published. It decreases our awareness. Not having proper education on book how publishing actually works prohibits us from building the confidence necessary to successfully start and run a publishing company. The lack of guidance, resources and experience add to our ignorance on book publishing and force us to think that the only way to see our writing in print is by taking the plunge of the traditional book publishing route. Ignorance is a disease that has a cure- but for many it is not known It is not known because they lack desire.

If this is you, you should seek either a literary agent or entertainment/literary attorney that will shop (pitch) your manuscript to book publishers. A literary agent will get anywhere from 5% to 25% of either your gross or net income from future book sells. If you use a literary agent to shop your manuscript to book publishers, you will still need a literary attorney to review and/or draft a contract on your behalf. A literary attorney will charge anywhere from $200/hr to $500/hr. Some literary attorneys have great connections in the book publishing business and may shop your book for you. In this case you may not need the services of a literary agent and may save yourself a few pennies. **If you seek the approval of a literary agent and want to take the traditional book-publishing business model, then stop reading now; this book is not for you!**

Are you seeking 50% to 100% of the retail-selling price from the book you authored? Do you want your writing and publishing generating efforts to free your from your 9 to 5 job? Are you seeking the fast track to wealth creation and retention through the formation of LLC's (limited liability companies) or other types of corporations? Are you seeking to maintain control and ownership of your intellectual property (i.e. copyrights that may generate hundreds of thousands if not millions of dollars over the life of the copyright which could be considered the life of the creator/writer/author (you) plus seventy some odd years)? A copyright is intellectual property and may be put into your financial portfolio, included in your will, trust or estate.

Are you seeking total control on the output of your book cover, spine and back panel? Do you want to cherry pick your editor who may be familiar with your personality, writing style and vision for your book? Do you have a number of titles you want to bring to market quickly instead of waiting for the approval of someone else? Do you have a unique marketing and promotions campaign that is unconventional, but you know will work, given you are able to work it? Are you ready to share your story, novel, fiction, non-fiction, how to resource guide or children's book with the world? Would you like to convert your paperback or hardback book into an audio or e-book, generating even more exposure for your works and profits for your pockets? Do you like the thought of being able to sell your book anywhere, anytime and anyplace in addition to selling your book through Borders, Barnes & Noble, Books-A-Million and Amazon.com? **Continue reading this book- it's designed with you in mind.**

Your story is too important to continue collecting dust in the basement, attic or garage. Your story is too important to wait for another publishing house's approval. Your story is too important to wait for the approval of an agent. Your story is too important for you to let fear stop you from achieving your goals and realizing your success.

Do as you were meant to do; take control of your own destiny and fulfill your dreams of becoming a published author. Your book may save a life, inspire another and bring you unparalleled happiness... but only if you take action today!

I am JaWar, author of the fastest selling music business book in Atlanta, the Atlanta Music Industry Connection, Resources for Artists, Producers and Managers. I was making less than $10/hour, working no more than 24 hours a week when the first edition of the Atlanta Music Industry Connection Book was published. As a child, I had a serious speech impediment (I stuttered) which made it very challenging for me to speak in public. Today, I conduct workshops and seminars on the business of music and book publishing. I consult businesses and individuals *just like you* on how to publish their fiction, non-fiction and technical books. This book should serve as a stepping-stone, resource guide and how to directory for your publishing efforts. Writers, authors, editors, publishers and anyone involved in the book publishing process will find this book useful. It is especially designed for someone seeking to bring their book to market or start their own publishing company.

"If I can do it so can you!" JaWar

WHO STOLE MY COPYRIGHTS?

As you read the story below you will know why you first need to cover your ass, by properly registering your intellectual property with the U.S. Library of Congress and have written agreements in place before doing anything concerning your book.

I had come to know a fairly prominent figure in the community and the hip hop music business as he is a member of a legendary hip hop group. This gentleman would come to know me in passing via community related events. Our paths would cross during the course of any given day in Atlanta. I asked this gentleman to be a panelist at one of my Music Therapy 101 Music Conferences and he accepted the offer. Some time had past and the gentleman contacted me via email and asked if I was interested in working on a project with him. I was excited about the opportunity and said yes I was interested. We met at Gladys's Chicken & Waffles off of Peachtree Street in Atlanta. I had two orders off collard greens and cornbread.

In any event we had lunch and the gentleman told me that he would often come in contact, as I might, with aspiring recording artist, producers and managers and that he wanted to help while helping himself at the same time. His idea was to create a pamphlet of contacts in Atlanta that would give folks resources that would help them pursue their dreams. The pamphlet would be something that was very easy to create and could be duplicated at a local print shop such as Kinko's. It sounded like a great idea and was right on time. You see for the past few years my company, the Music Industry Connection, LLC, published a free quarterly music industry newspaper. The paper contained articles about the business of music and various contacts in the music industry.

This new venture seemed very advantageous for several reasons. First, I saw a window of opportunity to build upon a business venture I'd already begun. Second, I would have a partner who would share in the responsibilities of making a business venture a success. Third, I was approached by a member of a legendary hip hop group to do business, so I knew this was going to help me move forward and that the person was serious.

During our next few meetings we discussed the pamphlet outline, marketing and distribution channels and street date we would begin selling the pamphlet. I immediately began creating a database of music industry contacts in Atlanta and considered how they would be organized in an easy to read fashion. In addition, I saw an opportunity to add value to the pamphlet by including previous released articles I had written for numerous publications including my own, the Music Industry Connection Newspaper. Such articles included "How to Market Your Independent Release" and "How to Use Record Pools to Test-Market Your Next Hit."

There were three interviews conducted that would be added to the pamphlet as well. The interviews would be of Al & Dayo of Own Music, Earle Holder, Mastering & Music Software Engineer and one of my then business partner. Al & Dayo of Own Music was my contact and I was introduced to Earle Holder through my business partner. I conducted the interviews and all three were video-taped by my former business partner. As the project began to take shape and form I started educating myself on the book publishing industry and found that we could produce a retail ready industry standard book for about the same price we were going to produce the pamphlet. I shared the exciting news with my former business partner. We adjusted our original outline and were even more motivated in creating this work. Soon after we received the proof copies of books to give us an idea of what the finished product would look like. The proofs would allow us to see what final adjustments we needed to make prior to our first print. We both *over*stood that the book would need changes and this would afford us the opportunity.

Shortly thereafter, we found that we differed on various aspects of the project. We began going back and forth on a number of issues including whose name should be read first on the book, if we should include pictures of ourselves and, if so, how these pictures should look. In addition, we started to express our differences related to what additional content should be included in the book. As time went on there were subtle changes in our business dealings. One of the most important changes was in our line of communication. I found that the more our communication broke down- the greater the differences we had in the direction of our book. The climate began to turn for the worse and I agreed only to meet with my former business partner in person if we had a moderator. We agreed on an entertainment attorney in Atlanta who we both had a mutual respect for both as a businessperson and community activist. As good measure I suggested that Earle Holder attend the initial meeting, since my former business partner introduced me to him. We had an informal meeting in a park in Atlanta and discussed many of the issues and miscommunication that had taken place. It appeared as though we might be able to resolve our differences and finish the book. However, towards the end of the meeting it became apparent that my former business partner was still hesitant with continuing the project.

It was suggested that my former business partner and I take some time and evaluate were the project was and have a final meeting to decide the direction of the book, we agreed. A few weeks later my former business partner, the entertainment attorney and I had another meeting in the same park. Earle Holder was not at this meeting. After meeting with my former business partner, he decided that he no longer wanted do business with me. As the project was nearly complete, I truly wanted to resolve our issues and move forward with publishing the book. I knew we had a dynamic product that would impact the lives of others. However, given my former business partners attitude toward the book, I agreed that we should go our separate ways.

Fortunately for us, we had an entertainment attorney present to give us some direction and closure on the legal issues. I was concerned about my intellectual property as I had written the majority of the book. We verbally agreed to some basic terms. I agreed not to release my book until two to three months after my formal business partner's book was published as he would have to create virtually a whole new book (I'd contributed 95% or more of the articles, essays and short questions in the book). I also agreed not to use the interviews that I did with he and Earle Holder, nor the illustrations that my former business partner provided for the book.

My former business partner agreed not to use any of my intellectual property, which included my articles, essays and short questions. He agreed not to use my interview with Al & Dayo of Own Music and to give me credit as the interviewer in his book for the interviews I conducted with he and Earle Holder.

These terms seemed pretty straightforward. Some time had passed and I saw my former business partner's book for sale at Earwax Records in Atlanta. I purchased a copy as I was eager to see what his vision would look like in print. To my surprise, *my former business partner had used every article, essay and short question that I contributed to the book!* To illustrate my point: in the third paragraph of the Producers Workshop Chapter of the *Atlanta Music Industry Connection* Book it reads, **"I know an entertainment attorney that was renting an apartment complex in Atlanta."** The sentence is written in first person, meaning the writer is the "doer" of the action i.e. I am the person who knows the entertainment attorney! What makes this compelling is my former business partner had the same sentence word-for-word in his book. The interesting part is that I didn't name the entertainment attorney in the book, so if you were to ask my former business partner who the entertainment attorney is whose apartment complex burned down- he would not know. The entertainment attorney that I am speaking of does not personally know my former business partner and knows him solely as being a member of a legendary hip hop group.

There is an article in the first edition of the *Atlanta Music Industry Connection: Resources for Artists, Producers, Managers* Book I wrote entitled "How to Use Record Pools to Test-Market Your Next Hit." Toward the end of the article I wrote, **"the record pool list is available in both a print and CD E-Book version. You may order your list of over 130 record pools by completing and mailing in the order-form at the end of this book."** My former business partner included the same article in his book word-for-word with the exception of the bold text above. Interestingly enough, I had been selling the record pool list years prior to writing the *Atlanta Music Industry Connection: Resources for Artists, Producers, Managers* Book. I would imagine my former business partner intentionally left out that you could order a copy of the record pool list, because he does not have the list to sell.

> *SPECIAL NOTE: By the time this book is printed I would have published a new book entitled Music Industry Connection: The Truth about Record Pools & Music Conferences, Talent Shows & Open Mics. In this book I give the most comprehensive directory of United States Record Pools and Music Conferences currently available in print.*

After reading my former business partners book I mailed him a certified letter with a return receipt. The letter included what I have shared with you. It also gave every page number and article, essay or question title where my material was used without permission in his book. In his book, my former business partner states that the articles where printed with permission. However, he was not granted permission to print any of my intellectual property. In fact much of the information that is being used in my former business partner's book is an act of copyright infringement, plagiarism, theft and unethical business practices. To this day I have not received any credit and, more importantly, any royalty checks for my work.

The moral to the story is to cover your ass, by properly registering your intellectual property with the U.S. Library of Congress and have written agreements in place before doing much of anything concerning your book or any other business transaction, no matter how well you think you know someone.

WHAT IS A COPYRIGHT?

A copyright is the natural protection of some intellectual property such as lyrics, music, songs, books, articles, essays and so forth. While not necessary in providing copyright protection for your work, you may still want to include either the word "copyright" or the c with a circle around it (i.e. ©) along with the copyright holders name in your body of work. On the back of this book, you will see the copyright year JaWar.

HOW DO YOU SECURE A COPYRIGHT?

When you affix your idea in some tangible form, it is automatically copyrighted. However, registering your copyright with the U.S. Library of Congress in a timely fashion affords you certain damages should someone knowingly infringe upon your intellectual property.

WHAT COPYRIGHT FORMS ARE NEEDED?

You will need copyright Form TX to register your book with the U.S. Library of Congress.

HOW DO I GET COPYRIGHT FORMS?

You may get copyright forms through from the United States Library of Congress. You can call or write to request the forms or you may visit their website download and print the forms for instant gratification. The Copyright Office contact details are below:

> ➤ Library of Congress, Copyright Office, Register of Copyrights, 101 Independence Avenue, S.E., Washington, D.C. 20559-6000
> P) 202-707-3000 P) 202-707-9100 F) 202-707-2600
> www.loc.gov/copyright

WHAT'S THE REGISTERING PRICE?

When this book was written it cost $45 to register a copyright with the Library of Congress. You may register a body (collection) of works under one title for the same price ($45) as long as the author of all the works are the same. If Paul and Janae each wrote a book they would have to individually pay $45 to register their copyright. If Paul and Janae wrote three books together they could register all three books under the same title, for instance Paul and Janae Volume 2 Books for the same $45. They could register all three books under the same title because the author(s) are the same for all of the books.

GET YOUR PAPER RIGHT

DO I NEED A BUSINESS LICENSE OR TAX I.D.?

Yes, you will need both a business license and tax I.D. to establish your business entity separate from your personal banking account(s). This will ensure that personal and business expenses and revenue generated are not commingled. For instance, a personal checking account should be different from a business checking account.

HOW DO I GET A BUSINESS LICENSE?

Normally, a business license may be obtained by contacting the local or county tax office. In most instances this information may be found either on the Internet through your favorite search engine, in the Local Yellow Pages or by contacting 411/directory assistance. To do an Internet search for the local or county tax office in the place you will be doing business, simply type in the name of the city or county with business license or tax office (Atlanta Business License or Los Angeles County Tax Office) in your favorite search engine. You may have to adjust the wording until you get the desired results.

Your public library may also be able to assist you with getting contact details to your local business license division. I have found the public library to be of great benefit, especially when the employees there become familiar with you and your project. They really tend to go the extra mile. At all cost, you will want to maintain a great working relationship with your local librarians. They are service providers and often will connect you with a number of people who also frequent the public library.

WHAT IS A TAX I.D.?

An EIN (Employer Identification Number) sometimes called a (FIN) Federal Identification Number is used to identify business entities. If you are starting a Partnership, LLC (Limited Liability Company) or Corporation you will need to apply for an EIN through the I.R.S. at www.irs.gov.

HOW DO I GET A TAX I.D.?

To obtain a tax I.D. (EIN/FIN) contact the I.R.S. at www.irg.gov. You will need to complete the SS-4 Form.

BUSINESS LICENSE AND TAX I.D.

A business license grants you the right to legally do business in your city or county. A Federal Employer Identification Number (Tax I.D.) is used to identify your business entity with the I.R.S (Internal Revenue Service).

WHAT IS AN ISBN NUMBER?

ISBN stands for International Standard Book Number and is used to uniquely identify every book. To ensure your book conforms to professional book publishing standards you will need to get an ISBN Number for all the books you publish in various formats. One of my book titles is called the Atlanta Music Industry Connection. If I published the book as a soft cover (paperback), hardcover, e-book and audio book I would need four different ISBN Numbers for each version of the book. Of course, any new editions or revisions for your books should have its' own ISBN Number. Retailers, wholesalers, distributors, libraries and readers may all refer to an ISBN Number when attempting to find a book title.

Your ISBN Number should be used to generate the barcode for your book. Your barcode should be placed on the bottom right hand corner on the back cover of your book. The price should either be embedded with the barcode or appear right above it. This has become the industry standard and makes it easy for book retailers, wholesalers, distributors and librarians to find pricing details. Take a look at your personal books, visit the local bookstore or library and see if what I am saying holds true for most books you check out.

HOW DO I GET AN ISBN NUMBER?

You may contact R.R. Bowker at www.bowker.com or call 888-269-5372 and ask for the ISBN application to get an ISBN Number. As of the writing of this book you would have to get a minimum of ten ISBN Numbers. The official United States Agency to get an ISBN Number is through R.R. Bowker and no other source. This will ensure your publishing house receives credit when your book is sold through traditional national chain bookstores.

HOW DO I GET A BARCODE?

Your book should have a Bookland EAN Barcode. This barcode is the book publishing industry standard and includes the pricing in the barcode. Your barcode should appear in the bottom right hand corner of your book. There are a number of companies in most states that will create a barcode for you using your ISBN. I have only listed a few companies particularly because of their ease of use and quick turn around time when processing through the Internet. I'd suggest doing a search to find the company that best suites your needs.

➤ Bar Code Graphics, Inc.
   1125 Eagle Park Road, Birmingham, AL 35242
   P) 800-662-0701
   www.barcode-us.com
   sales@barcode-us.com

➤ Fineline Technologies
   157 Technology Parkway, Suite 700, Norcross, GA 30092
   P) 678-969-0835 P) 800-500-8687 F) 678-969-9201
   www.finelinetech.com
   sales@finelinetech.com

➤ Fotel, Inc.
   1125 E. Saint Charles Road, Suite 100, Lombard, IL 60148
   P) 630-932-7520 P) 800-834-4920 F) 630-932-7610
   www.fotel.com
   coding@fotel.com

➤ General Graphics
   1608 Leishman Ave., P.O, Box 3192, Arnold, PA 15608
   P) 724-337-1470 P) 800-887-5894 F) 724-337-6589
   www.ggbarcode.com
   sales@ggbarcode.com

➤ Matthews International Corporation
   252 Park West Drive, Pittsburgh, PA 15275
   P) 412-249-2124 P) 800-245-1129 F) 412-788-2298

➤ Par Code Symbology, Inc.
   1275 Bloomfield Ave., Building 3-54, Fairfield, NJ 07004
   P) 973-227-5332 P) 800-524-0599 F) 973-575-4718

www.parcode.com
dave@parcode.com

> Swing Labels, LLC
  410 Great Road, Suite B9, Littleton, MA 01460
  P) 978-486-3200 F) 978-486-3087
  www.swinglabels.com
  jcannon@swinglabels.com

> The Bureau of Engraving
  3400 Technology Drive, Minneapolis, MN 55418
  P) 800-786-8727 F) 800-786-8734
  www.thebureau.com
  bureau@earthlink.net

WHAT IS A U.P.C. NUMBER & BARCODE?

U.P.C. stands for Universal Product Code and is issued by the U.C.C. the Uniform Code Council. Every industry has a unique set of U.P.C. Numbers assigned to it. These numbers are pre-determined. After applying for a U.P.C. Number your company will be given a set of numbers that it may use to create specific numbers for every product in its' catalog. Unless you have a mass-market paperback normally sold in grocery stores, you probably will not need a U.P.C. Number and Barcode.

HOW MAY I GET A U.P.C. BARCODE?

> U.C.C. – Uniform Code Council
  Customer Service 7887
  Washington Village Dr., Suite 300, Dayton, OH 45459
  P) 937-435-3870 F) 937-435-7317
  www.uc-council.org
  info@uc-council.org

LCCN: LIBRARY CONGRESS CONTROL NUMBER

A Library of Congress Control Number or LCCN is different from a copyright. A copyright protects your intellectual property should someone infringe upon your rights, steals your work or plagiarizes your material. Libraries and other buyers may locate, select and order your books using an LCCN. Having an LCCN is helpful, but not necessary for getting your book into the public library system. Given the number of titles available every year on any number of subjects you should not hesitate to get an LCCN.

HOW DO I GET A LCCN?

Get a Library Congress Control Number by contacting the Cataloging in Publication Division at the Library of Congress at 202-707-6372 or visit http://pcn.loc.gov/pcn to apply online. It is very important to apply for your LCCN three to six weeks prior to printing and publishing your book, because the LCCN needs to be printed on the copyright page of your book and may take a few weeks before you receive it.

PROTECTING YOUR PUBLISHING COMPANY

To ensure you protect your publishing companies name and logo you will want to apply for a trademark with your local Secretary of State. Any Secretary of State Office may be found by looking in your favorite search engine on the Internet. For instance, you may type Secretary of State Georgia or Secretary of State California. You may also contact 411 or directory assistance to help you. The public library may also serve as a great resource in helping you locate the Secretary of State.

U.S. PROTECTION FOR YOUR COMPANY

To protect your publishing companies name and logo in the United States, apply for a federal trademark or servicemark through the U.S. Patent & Trademark Office. One of the criterion for establishing your federal trademark is that no other individual, entity or company may own the rights to the mark. You must also be using the mark in more than one state to complete the registration process.

> ➤ U.S. Patent and Trademark Office
> General Information Services Division
> Crystal Plaza 3, RM 2 C02
> Washington, D.C. 20231
> P) 800-786-9199
> www.uspto.gov

WHAT IS DUN & BRADSTREET?

Dun & Bradstreet is a credit rating agency for businesses. It tracks the credit worthiness of businesses much like Equifax, Experian and Transunion tracks the credit worthiness of individuals.

HOW TO CONTACT DUN & BRADSTREET?

> ➤ D&B Corp., 103 JFK Pkwy, Short Hills, NJ 07078
> P) 800-234-3867
> custserv@dnb.com
> www.dnb.com

GETTING BOOK DISTRIBUTION

WHAT IS DISTRIBUTION?

Before we can "get distribution"- we must know what it is exactly. We must have a working knowledge on what it means to us. Distribution is when you move your product from production or manufacturing to the end-users hand, hard-drive, cell phone or whatever medium allows them to take possession of what you are selling (in this case your book.) In short: Distribution is getting your book from the printer to the reader.

Distribution may take different form. For instance, you may distribute your book over the Internet electronically. This would mean that your book would need to be an e-book and available in a PDF or other widely used format. PDF is a software application that allows for the compression of different documents such as a Microsoft Word documents.

Many writers, authors, editors, printers, publishers and retailers believe distribution to mean that your book is sold in a major chain store. The idea that distribution means having your book sold in major chains is what prevents many writers, authors and small size publishers from doing it themselves. In order to succeed as an independent publisher, you must revise your thinking and know that you have the ability to do what many have done and will continue to do.

When you get your books from the printer and put them on consignment at the independent bookstore in your city- you have distributed your book! When you sell your books at wholesale directly to a specialty store- you have distributed your books. When you sell books after your lecture, seminar or workshop to attendees you have distributed your book. When someone visits your website, purchases your book online with a credit card using paypal or some other merchant service and you ship the book to that customer- you have distributed your book. When someone buys a download of your e-book from your website- you have distributed your book. Granted there are various levels and sophistication of distribution. As an independent writer, author and publisher you can do it as I have demonstrated above. By doing it yourself you will learn so much in the process. You will be forced to be organized, communicate effectively, keep accurate and complete records and learn what it means to have distribution.

Independent distribution is a fantastic way to create, maintain and grow a consistent cash flow. With independent distribution you are able to generate revenue (money) instantly, daily, weekly, monthly, quarterly and so on. Remember when you move your book from production or the printer to the end-users possession you have achieved distribution. You will always want to have a few books in your car, home or office to take advantage of opportunities as they become available.

CREATING A DISTRIBUTION SYSTEM

You will want to create an internal distribution system for your books. This will consider the end user or readers and everyone in the middle of the process that makes it possible for the readers to get your books in the most convenient and time efficient manner feasible. Your distribution system should consider the completion time of production, the time it takes to transport your product from the printer to you, the wholesaler, distributor, retailer or customer. You will need to closely monitor how many books you order, how fast they sell to who, when and where. This will help you gage when to order more books and at what quantity. As an independent or self-publisher you will most likely use a shipping service such as UPS or FEDEX to transport your books. Make sure you know their policy on shipping, insurance and so forth. These things become extremely important if you are planning a big event and need your books available by a certain date.

Keep in mind when you get your books from the printer and take them to the stores you become an active participant in the shipping process. During the initial stages of your budding publishing company you may be doing much of the running around. As your business begins to grow you will want to consider bringing someone on board to help with this task. Ask yourself, how responsible does someone have to be to deliver books to stores, how much time does it take and what else may be required of the person. These are just some of the questions you will need to ask someone before hiring them.

INTERNET DISTRIBUTION

As an independent publisher, or self-published author, the Internet is one of the best tools you have for continued marketing and selling of your books. Some of the things you will need to take advantage of Internet distribution are your own website or domain name. Some of my domain names are **gojawar.com** and **makemoneyselfpublishing.com**. Your site should be clean, professional and maintain a consistent look throughout. There is little need to have a site that is flash intense. Visitors want what they want fast. They want a site that is easy to navigate, includes contact details/information on the author and book(s) and how to buy. Many people are familiar with paypal as a payment solutions provider and use it to process and accept credit card payments online. You may visit www.paypal.com to get details about accepting credit card payments on your site. Additional payment solutions may be found by typing "online payment solutions", "internet merchant accounts" or "internet credit card processors", etc. in your favorite search engine.

Having and selling your book(s) from your own website is fantastic as it allows you to maintain the majority of the profits and have direct contact with your buyers. In addition, to selling your book from your own website, you will want to use the popular social websites of the day to locate and promote to new readers and convert them into paying clients. Some of today's popular social sites include myspace.com, facebook.com, myfve.com and youtube.com. Keep your eyes and ears open, as these popular sites tend to change every few years for a number of reasons. You want to ensure you have your hand on "the pulse" and find these sites before they get saturated. Maximizing these social sites means monitoring the visitors to your page, participating in online discussion groups, posting blogs, comments and sending mass-messages to people in your internal group regularly. Whenever possible you will want to include a link that will forward people from your social site to a place where they may buy your book(s). This may include a buy now paypal button, a link to the amazon.com page that shows your book on directly to your own website. Remember: your goal by being an active participant on social websites is to inform and convert. Inform people of who you are and the book(s) you have written and convert them into buying customers.

Another avenue of internet distribution is through affiliate programs. An "affiliate program" simply means giving another person or site a commission whenever books are sold through that persons website. The program is mutually beneficial for several reasons. First, you get optimum exposure on a number of websites without having to invest additional money for marketing. Because the person needs to bring awareness of your book to convince and convert book buyers to purchase; they are encouraged to actively market on their site. Second, because the transaction is pass-through in nature, your affiliate client does not have to invest in any inventory, they are not required to buy books upfront or stock books in a warehouse. The affiliate will have an image, price and information on your book. When someone clicks the buy now button they are forwarded to a unique page you set up where your book may be bought. This page will be set-up specifically for this affiliate member and/or have a special code that will let you know what affiliate sent you the sale. Once the book buyer purchases the book you will forward payment to the affiliate member. This process may sound complicated, but it is not. However, there are companies that will facilitate your affiliate program from start to end for a fee. For details on these company's, type "affiliate programs" in your favorite search engine.

WEBSITES TO SELL YOUR BOOKS

There are a few ways to get your books sold through large bookstores online. One way is to have your book distributed through a large distributor or wholesaler and ensure your book is in their system for ordering. When someone places an order through one of the online bookstores your distributor or wholesaler will send you an invoice for "X" number of books. You will ship them the quantity of books ordered. Once they get the books they will enter them into their system and ship them either directly to the customer or to the online bookstore. The online bookstore will then ship the book to the book buyer. The quicker you get the book to your distributor or wholesaler, the quicker the book buyer gets your book and the quicker you receive payment for books shipped.

Another way of having your books sold through one of the major bookstores online is to visit the websites below and look for something on the site that reads "independent book seller/publisher" or "how to sell your books on our site." Simply follow the instructions word for word and your book will be made available for the public to view and buy. Typically, the bookstores will not order books from you until they see a *demand* meaning people are actually buying your books from them. Once that happens, they may purchase a small quantity of books from you. I have found that once your book is available on amazon.com, bn.com, borders.com and booksamillion.com it then is available on a host of other online stores. Many stores you didn't know existed. I imagine these sites are tied into the larger stores online inventory system. It is virtual distribution at work and you are the benefactor.

Seeing your book(s) on amazon.com, bn.com, borders.com and booksamillion.com is a great ego booster for first time authors and publishers. It also gives you a since of credibility to book buyers. As a publisher you are in the business of selling books. As an author you are in the business of selling information- be it fiction, non-fiction, reference or otherwise. The point is while it is great psychologically to see your books on major bookstores websites you are sharing the profits with someone else. Your long-term plan should be to draw traffic to your website and convert those visitors to buying clients. This way you are able to keep the lion's share of the profit. More importantly, by having people buy books from your website, you are able to retain important data such as emails, names and phone numbers, etc. that allow you to "upsell" other books and merchandise you make available to customers. It is easier to sell to an existing customer than a new one.

- www.amazon.com
- www.bn.com
- www.borders.com
- www.booksamillion.com

DISTRIBUTORS

➢ A & B Distributors
1000 Atlantic Avenue, Brooklyn, NY 11238
P) 718-783-7808

➢ Afrikan World Books
2217 Penn Ave., Box 16447, Baltimore, MD 21217
P) 410-728-0877

➢ Biblio Distribution
4720 Boston Way, Lanham, MD 20706
P) 301-459-3366 F) 301-459-1705

➢ Book Tech Distributing
5961 E. 39th Ave., Denver, CO 80207
P) 800-758-5492 P) 303-329-0300 F) 303-329-3117

- ➢ Client Distribution Services
  425 Madison Ave., Suite 1500, New York, NY 10017
  P) 212-223-2969 F) 212-223-1504
  www.cdsbooks.com

- ➢ Consortium Book Sales & Distribution
  1045 Westgate Dr., St. Paul, MN 55114
  P) 800-283-3572 P) 651-221-9035 F) 651-221-0124
  www.cbsd.com
  consortium@cbsd.com

- ➢ Culture Plus Books
  291 Livingston Street, Brooklyn, NY 11217
  P) 718-222-9309

- ➢ D & J Distributors
  229-21B Merrick Boulevard, Laurelton, NY 11413
  P) 718-949-5400 P) 718-949-6161

- ➢ Distributed Art Publishers
  155 Sixth Ave., 2nd Floor, New York, NY 10013
  P) 212-627-1999 F) 212-627-9484

- ➢ Educational Book Distributors
  P.O. Box 551, San Mateo, CA 94401
  P) 650-344-8458 F) 650-344-7840

- ➢ Koens Book Distributors
  10 Twosome Drive, Moorestown, NJ 08057
  P) 800-257-8481

- ➢ Parnassus Book Distributors
  200 Academy Way, Columbia, SC 29206
  P) 800-782-7760 P) 803-782-7748 F) 803-782-7748

- ➢ Partners Book Distributors
  2325 Jarco Drive, P.O. Box 580, Holt, MI 48842
  P) 800-336-3137

- Quality Books
  1003 West Pines Rd., Oregon, IL, 61061
  P) 815-732-4450 F) 815-732-4499
  www.quality-books.com

- Rights & Distribution, Inc.
  2131 Hollywood Blvd., Suite 305, Hollywood, FL 33020
  P) 800-771-3355 P) 954-925-0555 F) 954-925-5244
  www.fellpub.com

- SCB Distributors
  15608 S. New Century Dr., Gardena, CA 90248
  P) 800-729-6423 P) 310-532-9400 F) 310-532-7001
  www.scbdistributors.com
  info@scbdistributors.com

- Small Press Distribution
  1341 Seventh St., Berkeley, CA 94710
  P) 800-869-7553 P) 510-524-1668 F) 510-524-0852
  www.spdbooks.org
  orders@spdbooks.org

- Spring Arbor Distributors
  One Ingram Blvd., LaVergne, TN 37086
  P) 800-395-5599 F) 734-483-3675
  www.springarbor.com
  info@springarbor.com

- Unique Books
  5010 Kemper Ave., St. Louis, MO 63139
  P) 800-533-5446 F) 800-916-2455

- Words Distributing Co.
  7900 Edgewater Dr., Oakland, CA 94621
  P) 800-593-9673 F) 510-553-0729
  www.wordsdistributing.com
  words@wordsdistributing.com

BOOK WHOLESALERS

Book wholesalers provide a similar function as book distributors. Essentially, they both act as mediums to getting books into major chain and independent bookstores, specialty shops and libraries. Traditionally, distributors would have sales reps that would solicit book to their clients, while wholesalers would simply ship books to clients who placed orders with them. As the book publishing industry becomes increasingly competitive, some distributors may be less likely to promote their clients books to stores and libraries. As a self-published author you cannot afford to leave success up to chance or in the hands of someone else. You must take the drivers seat and constantly build your brand, promote your book and publicize its' release. Below are a list of book wholesalers. Two of the largest book wholesalers are Ingram and Baker & Taylor. Visit their websites or call them for details about what you need to do to have them carry your book. Remember to tell them JaWar, Author of How to Self-Publish for Profit sent you.

> ➤ Academic Book Center
> 5600 NE Hassalo St., Portland, OR 97213
> P) 800-547-7704 P) 503-287-6657 F) 503-284-8859

> ➤ Ambassador Book Service
> 42 Chasner St., Hempstead, NY 11550
> P) 800-431-8913 P) 516-489-4011 F) 516-489-5661
> www.absbook.com
> ambassador@absbook.com

> ➤ Baker & Taylor
> Publishers Service Department
> P.O. Box 6885, Bridgewater, NJ 08807

www.btol.com

➤ Blackwell's Book Services
  100 University Court, Blackwood, NJ 08012
  P) 800-257-7341 P) 856-228-8900 F) 856-228-7672
  www.blackwell.com

➤ Bookazine Corporation
  75 Hook Rd., Bayoone, NJ 07002
  P) 800-221-8112 P) 201-339-7777 F) 201-339-7778
  www.bookazine.com

➤ Book House, Inc.
  208 West Chicago St., Jonesville, MI 49250
  P) 800-248-1146 P) 517-849-2117 F) 517-849-9716
  www.thebookhouse.com
  bhinfo@thebookhouse.com

➤ Bookpeople
  7900 Edgewater Dr. Oakland, CA 94621
  P) 510-632-4700 F) 510-632-1281
  www.bponline.com
  bpeople@bponline.com

➤ Brodart Company
  500 Arch St., Williamsport, PA 17701
  P) 800-233-8567 P) 570-326-2461 F) 800-999-6799
  www.brodart.com

➤ Coutts Library Service
  P.O. Box 1000, Niagara Falls, NY 14302
  P) 800-772-4304 P) 716-282-8627 F) 716-282-3831
  www.coutts-ls.com

➤ Devorss and Company
  P.O. Box 550, Marina Del Rey, CA 90294
  P) 310-822-8940 F) 310-821-6290
  www.devorss.com

- The Distributors
  702 South Michigan, South Bend, IN 46601
  P) 800-348-5200 P) 219-232-8500 F) 312-577-0440
  www.thedistributors.com
  info@thedistributors.com

- Eastern Book Company
  131 Middle St., Portland, ME 04101
  P) 800-937-0331 P) 207-774-0331 F) 207-774-4678
  www.ebc.com
  info@ebc.com

- Emery-Pratt Company
  1966 West Main St., Owosso, MI 48867
  P) 517-723-5291 F) 517-723-4677
  www.emery-pratt.com
  office@emery-pratt.com

- Ingram Book Company
  One Ingram Blvd, LaVergne, TN 37086
  P) 800-937-8100 F) 615-793-5000
  www.ingrambook.com

- Midwest Library Service
  11443 St. Charles Rock Rd., Bridgeton, MO 63044
  P) 314-739-3100
  www.midwestls.com
  all@midwestls.com

- National Association of College Stores
  528 East Lorain St., Oberlin, OH 44074
  P) 800-321-3883 P) 440-775-7777 F) 800-344-5059
  www.nacscorp.com

- The News Group
  3900-A Industrial Drive E., Fife, WA 98424
  P) 253-922-8011 F) 253-896-5027

- ➢ Nutri-Books/Royal Publications
  P.O. Box 5793, Denver, CO 80217
  P) 303-778-8383 F) 303-744-9383

- ➢ Sunbelt Publications
  1250 Fayette St., El Cajon, CA 92020
  P) 800-626-6579 P) 619-258-4911 F) 619-258-4916
  www.sunbeltpub.com
  subbeltpub@prodigy.net

- ➢ YBP Library Services
  999 Maple St., Contoocook, NH 03339
  P) 800-258-3774 P) 603-746-3102 F) 603-746-5628
  www.ybp.com
  service@tbp.com

WHAT IS A ONE-SHEET?

A one-sheet is an industry standard document used to inform retailers, distributors, wholesalers and other buyers about a new release. A one-sheet should be clean with little clutter, easy to read, a large display of the book cover, the ISBN Number, ordering details and noteworthy endorsements. Your one-sheet should be on full color paper. Keep in mind this paper acts as your sells sheet, especially if you are not there to pitch (sell) the person on the book. One-sheets are used for both Book and CD releases. A one-sheet contains the following:

- ➢ Book or CD Cover Artwork
- ➢ ISBN/Barcode Number
- ➢ Suggested retail price
- ➢ Wholesale price
- ➢ Book distributor contact details for ordering product
- ➢ Special author mention (e.g. newsworthy awards or a fantastic review from an established author in the genre.)

RETAIL STORES

For several months I actively marketed the first edition of the Atlanta Music Industry Connection Book. I promoted the book directly to my target market. I went to music conferences, talents shows and industry networking events. Anywhere my target reader was, so was I. I distributed flyers telling people stores at which the book was available. I also sent email blasts twice a month with excerpts and useful information for my readers about the music industry from my book at the end of the email. I would tell them what stores were selling the *Atlanta Music Industry Connection*.

One day I decided to call one of the larger chain music retail stores in Atlanta in an effort to get my book sold there. While it would have been great if the store bought the books outright, I was more concerned with getting the book in the store even if on consignment (consignment is fully discussed in the next section.) I knew the book would sell; it just needed to be available and visible. When I called the store I was put in touch with the consignment manager. When I introduced myself as JaWar, Author of the *Atlanta Music Industry Connection: Resources for Artists, Producers and Managers,* the consignment manager seemed extremely excited to hear from me. He said he had been meaning to contact me for weeks as the store had a number of people who were coming in requesting my book, this was not hype- this was *critical mass*. Hype is Hollywood, fluff, lights cameras, rumors and so forth. Hype has its' place in your branding, marketing and publicity efforts. Critical mass is the truth, the real, and the money. Critical mass demands attention- it calls to action. My hype machine had built itself into a frenzy of critical mass. This was evident by people going into the national music retail store chain requesting my book. It was witnessed by the excitement by the stores consignment manager when I called. It was further evident once the book was in the store and it started selling.

Getting your book sold in retail stores is simple if you've done your homework. Before approaching book and specialty stores you should have built a loyal following of readers. This is achieved by distributing flyers, getting book reviews and interviews in local and regional publications, having a website where readers can visit at their leisure to get updates on the author and sending regular emails to new and existing readers.

While building a loyal reader base, an author will want to build solid relationships with book retailers. Visit local independent and chain bookstores at least once a month and ask the manager or owner if your book's genre is selling well at their store. Ask what those authors are doing to create such a demand for their product. Ask the manager or owner for suggestions for creating a buzz for a new author and release. If you listen- you will learn far more than you would imagine. After doing these things you will know when it is time to put your book in stores. Your hype machine will be in full swing creating frenzy about your book; critical mass will begin to form!

GETTING PAID

> Upfront Money

- ➤ C.O.D. Money
- ➤ Invoice Money
- ➤ Consignment Money

"Upfront money" is when you are paid immediately by the store upon delivery of your books to the store. This money is given in the form of cash, money order or check. I like upfront money the best and I have a sense you will too. Because of cash flow restraints, inventory control and overhead; most stores will not purchase your books from you upfront, at least not initially. As your title or titles begin to sell stores may elect to buy your books outright.

When approaching a bookstore you will want to ask about the process of getting a new book or title in the store or specifically, "Who's responsible for ordering new books?" By the way: this question is *carefully worded.* It positions you to find out if the person you are speaking with is the person responsible for ordering books or not. If the person you are talking with is the one responsible for getting new books into the store they will tell you if they buy books upfront, are invoiced, buy on consignment, and, if so, whether its from a wholesaler or distributor. Remember it is the *carefully worded* question that positions you to get the information you need to get your books into a given store. More importantly, it helps you determine if you will get paid upfront from your books in a store.

As authors and publishers we are always delighted when our books are bought upfront. I always attempt to give stores a bonus when they purchase books upfront from me. This may mean referring people to their store on your website, promoting them in print and online advertisement when marketing your book, giving them free goods to sell from time to time and/or sending them special gifts or thank you cards, especially during the holiday season. Many times it is the smaller things that have a big impact and maintain favor with people.

Upfront money usually is the best money, especially for a new publisher. Upfront money allows you to maintain and increase your cash flow, take advantage of more advertising opportunities and pay recurring bills on time.

C.O.D. means "cash on delivery" and is a form of upfront money. C.O.D. is equivalent to using an escrow company. An escrow company is a third party that holds money until goods or services are delivered. To ship a package C.O.D. you would complete additional paperwork determining the amount of money that is to be collected from the receiver. This amount of money may or may not include the shipping cost- that is for you to decide. Once the person or store gets your package, they would pay the carrier and the carrier would return payment to you. C.O.D. may be used through the U.S. Postal Service. C.O.D. normally requires additional paperwork, but often is worth the effort to ensure prompt payment for books delivered.

I had also approached a media supply store about selling the *Music Industry Connection* book I published. Initially, they agreed to put six books in the store on consignment. After seeing that the six books would sell, the store allowed me to invoice them for twelve books when it was time to restock.

Invoice money is the next best thing to upfront money. Invoice money is when you deliver your books and receive payment some time in the future. Your payment may come in 30, 60, 90 or 120 days after your books are delivered to the store. As with upfront monies some stores may allow you to invoice them after they see there is a demand for your books. You will use the same *carefully worded* question (asking what the process is for getting a new book in the store or who is responsible for ordering new books) when attempting to find out if you may invoice a store for books delivered.

Invoice templates may be found in Microsoft Word or many of the other low cost software applications found in office supply stores like Staples and Office Depot. You may find free invoice templates on the Internet by conducting a search in your favorite search engine.

Your invoice should have some basic information. It should have the seller (your publishing company name, physical mailing address, phone, fax and email) the buyer (store), the date the books are delivered, title of the book, quantity (amount) of books delivered, the ISBN Number, a unique invoice number, payment terms and method. The payment terms may read NET 30, 60, 90 or 120 days. "NET 30 days" means your money should be sent within 30 days to you. Likewise "NET 60 or 90" means your money should be sent to you within 60 or 90 days from the date your books are delivered to the store. Ideally, you will want to have your payment sent within 30 days. The method terms would include where the money should be sent: be it a wire, money order or physical check. Most likely the payment will be sent via snail or first class postal mail as a check. Invoice money is great because you know you have money coming. Be mindful that you'll want to keep accurate records, as stores don't always honor invoice payments, not because they are attempting to keep your money, but they may not keep good records and may overlook timely payments. When you are on the receiving end of an invoice payment it is considered "accounts receivable." When you are on the sending end of a payment it is called "accounts payable." When contacting a store you have invoiced you will want to ask for their accounts payable department. Most boutique, small or independent bookstores, have one person handling all their accounting. Larger firms typically have accounts payable and accounts receivable departments, always ask to be sure. I have found it always better to be honest, sincere and friendly when attempting to correct an accounting error or to get money due to you from an invoiced client.

Consignment is where you leave your product (book, CDs, t-shirts, etc.) with the retailer to sell for a pre-determined price. For instance, you may sell your book to the store for $8.39 and the store may resell your book for $13.99. Once your book is actually sold to a customer, then you are due your $8.39 from the store. You are paid your money only after your product is sold. While it is always advantageous to get your money up front from retailers, most stores will choose to put your book on consignment. After your book has demonstrated a degree of success, some stores will opt to buy your books outright from you. Consignment works the same for books, CDs and t-shirts, etc.

To ensure that you don't miss any retail sales, I recommend you create two "call days" a month. Your call days will be a specific time and day that you will contact retail stores to get inventory details. For instance, you may call stores on the first and third Monday of every month between 10:00am and 12:00pm. During this call time you will simply ask the retailer how many books are currently in stock. For instance, during my call days I will contact the stores and say "Good Morning, I'm JaWar. Will you tell me how many copies of the *How to Self-Publish for Profit Books* you have left."

Call days help you achieve several things. First, they help you maintain a working relationship with retailers. Second, it demonstrates to the retailer that you are serious about your project and have a system for monitoring sales. Thirdly, by having call days you will know when it is time to visit the store to either sell them more books and/or collect your money from product left on consignment. This will help you control your inventory so that you know how much product to order and when. This will help you maintain better cash flow. Over time you'll know which stores are your "bulls" and which ones are your "bears." Bulls being the stores that sell the highest volume of your product and bears being the stores that sell the lowest volume of your product in a relative time period (i.e. over 30, 60 or 90 days.) Keep in mind that every sale is a product sold and at the end of the day it all adds up.

You will want to start contacting independent book and specialty stores in your local area first. An independent store is one that is not a national chain. Borders, Books-A-Million and Barnes & Noble are national chain stores. In Atlanta Nubian

Books or Medu Books would be considered local independent stores. A specialty store is one that is not a bookstore and may not regularly sell books, but would work great for your book. Because most of my books tend to be entertainment, (specifically music industry based) then a specialty store would be a music retail or music equipment store. If you wrote a book on how to build racetracks for R/C or remote control cars- a specialty store would be a hobby shack. If you wrote a book on alternative fuels, a specialty store may be a health food grocery store, since people who shop there may be interested in preserving the earth, living a healthier lifestyle and progressive in their thinking. Specialty stores are great additions to distributing your book beyond traditional bookstores as they immediately give you new opportunities for marketing and selling your work, often with less competition from similar books.

You should be able to locate independent bookstores in your city or town by typing in "local (your city's name) bookstores" in your favorite search engine, looking in the Yellow Pages, asking family, friends, co-workers and contacting others in your area using social websites such as myspace.com and myfve.com.

CHAIN BOOK STORES

> Barnes & Noble
> 122 Fifth Ave., 4th FL., New York, NY 10011
> P) 212-633-3300 F) 212-675-0413
> www.bn.com

> Books-A-Million
> 402 Industrial Lane, Birmingham, AL 35211

P) 800-201-3550 F) 205-942-3737
www.booksamillion.com

➢ Borders
100 Phoenix Dr., Ann Arbor, MI 48108
P) 800-770-7811 P) 734-913-1100 P) 734-477-1100
www.borders.com

ALTERNATIVE CHAIN BOOK STORES

➢ Costco Wholesale
999 Lake Dr., Issaquah, WA 98027
P) 425-313-8100
www.costco.com

➢ Target
33 South 6th St., Minneapolis, MN 55402
P) 800-440-0680 P) 612-304-8637 P) 612-304-7500
www.target.com

➢ Sam's Club
608 SW 8th St., Bentonville, AR 72716
P) 501-277-7160
www.walmart.com

BRANDING, PROMOTIONS AND PUBLICITY

BRANDING

Branding is the constant relaying of your message or corporate identity to your target market. You want to reiterate to potential and current readers your writing style and genre of interest. Branding is a 24/7 opportunity; it's not a 9 to 5 job. Approaching your branding efforts from this vantage point ensures you constantly are on people's minds. Most likely when you hear "we bring good things to life" you think of GE or General Electric. You think of GE when you hear "we bring good things to life" because they have branded those words- that image in our minds. They have fed us "we bring good things to life" so much many of us now believe that GE does, in fact, bring good things to life. Perception is reality.

When you think of Stephen King what type of writing do you think of? Do you think of love stories, romance novels, inspirational, relationship or music books? Your answer is undoubtedly none of the above. When you think of Stephen King you think of suspense, horror and mystery. Even when you see pictures or video of Stephen King he looks the part. Stephen must be well aware of branding and the need for him to play the part whenever in public view.

What type of writer are you? What comes natural or easy? What genre are you most comfortable and passionate about writing about? Now ask yourself? How will you constantly relay that brand of writing to potential and current readers? How will you be the Stephen King of your writing style when it comes to branding yourself and books? Your brand is your identity, especially when you are not there in person. Your brand may be seen or heard on business cards, flyers, letterhead, TV, radio and websites, etc.

PROMOTIONS

Promotions deals with the execution of your branding, marketing and publicity campaigns. Promotions entail sending email blast, distributing flyers, business cards, bookmarks, ink pens and other items promoting your book. You will want to use those tools that are best suited for your campaign. Be vigilant and plan for the long haul when it comes to your promotions effort.

PUBLICITY

Most people often don't have a clear understanding of publicity or public relations work. Often it is meshed with branding, marketing and promotions. While there is overlap in the subject matter, publicity is its' own field with a unique approach to helping you spread the word about your book and publishing company. Publicity has to do with relaying your story or message to media in an effort to get write-ups, interviews, reviews and overall mention of your book and company. By getting media interested in you and your book, you increase the opportunities for greater exposure to your target market through mass communication.

One of the best ways to secure media exposure is by having a compelling story in which the readers, viewers and listeners of various media outlets will be interested. Exposure to media outlets is normally achieved by sending a newsworthy press release. The tag line or heading for a press release is extremely important as it normally determines if the press release will be read in a timely fashion (if at all) by media. For example, "Robert T. Kiyosaki is to *Rich Dad Poor Dad* what JaWar is to *Music Industry Connection"* or "Donald Trump is to Real Estate what JaWar is to the Music Industry" may be compelling enough tag lines to cause media to read the entire press release. If the material is substantive for their readers they may rerun the story, write their own version or seek an interview.

GET FREE BUSINESS CARDS PRINTED

Go to www.vistaprint.com to get free business cards.

GETTING FLYERS PRINTED FOR FREE?

First, determine who may need to promote their business in the city. Remember the business does not necessarily have to be music related. For instance, a local clothing store, real estate agent or car dealership, may want to promote their business. Second, the business should be one that has the money, but not the time to distribute the flyers. Third, set up a meeting with the possible candidates. Fourth, let them know that you are an aspiring author, editor, publisher, etc. seeking a co-op (cooperative) opportunity to help spread the word about your businesses.

Propose that they get one side of the flyer to promote their business and that you get the other to promote yours. Next propose that they pay for the printing of the flyers and that you distribute them. Inform them that because your business is promoted on one-side of the flyer that you have a "VESTED INTEREST" in ensuring that the flyers are properly distributed.

Remember to use the words "VESTED INTEREST"- it has a very professional tone to it.

Before you approach any one, remember that your typed proposal has the following details: the printing company you will be using, the exact price for printing, shipping and taxes, if applicable, turnaround time (time it will take to get the flyers back) and your distribution points (drop-off locations). Below is a list of printers for your flyer needs. Remember to tell the JaWar, author of *How to Self-Publish for Profit Book* sent you.

> ➤ APG Media
>   2195 Defoor Hills Rd., Atlanta, GA 30318
>   P) 404-797-2880 F) 866-355-0834
>   apgmedia@aol.com

> ➤ Jakprints, Inc.
>   1300 West 78th St., Cleveland, OH 44102
>   P) 877-246-3132 P) 216-472-1650 F) 216-472-6349
>   www.jakprints.com

> ➤ PK Graphics
>   420 Lincoln Rd. Suite #305 Miami, Florida 33139
>   P) 305-534-2184 F) 305-534-8763
>   www.pkgraphics.com
>   mig@pkgraphics.com

USING THE INTERNET FOR FREE?

Most public libraries provide free internet access. Some even offer access to Microsoft Word, Excel and PowerPoint for typing letters, invoices, proposals and presentations, etc. You will find that each library has its on way of doing things, so check around, find the one that works best for you and start using the internet for free.

Other places that may offer free internet access are places of worship, the Goodwill, the Department of Labor and colleges & universities.

If you have a laptop with a wireless (wifi) card you can find a number of coffee houses, restaurants and car washes etc. that will offer free wireless internet access. A few cities in the U.S. have entire neighborhoods wired for free wireless access. Ask family, friends and co-workers if they know of any places you may use the internet for free from time to time. Their answers could shock you.

GETTING A FREE EMAIL ACCOUNT?

You may get a free email account at either www.yahoo.com, www.hotmail.com or www.gmail.com (google). There are other free email account systems, but these may be the most popular on the internet.

If you are serious about creating windows of opportunities for yourself in the book publishing business, you will need to have access to the internet and an email account. It is not up for debate.

PRINTERS FOR FLYERS & BOOKMARKS

Flyers are a cost-effective method for promoting your business or new book release and should be considered as one of your promotional tools. One of the best ways to ensure that you maximize your flyers potential is to include as much contact information on the flyer as possible. For instance, include two phone numbers, two emails, a website and physical mailing address. Your contact details do not have to be BIG, just large enough to be read. Remember, you want to make it easy for people to locate you in the event they want to order more books, hire you to speak, co-author a book and/or turn your book into a movie.

A gentleman contacted me about registering for my Music Therapy 101 Music Business Seminar. He said he had one of the flyers for about three years and was just now calling. Had I not included a working number on the flyer I would have missed a paying registrant for the upcoming Music Therapy 101 Music Seminar.

Some of the places that flyers may be distributed are book and specialty retail stores, publishing conferences, book festivals, libraries, barber-shops, beauty salons, high schools and college campuses. While not always practical, it is advisable to get permission before distributing your flyers at any of these locations or events. However, the truth is that sometimes you will have to take the guerilla marketing approach, go in like a Navy Seal, do your work (pass out flyers) and keep it moving.

I have been kicked out of malls, clubs, schools and special events for distributing flyers and selling my CDs, but by the time I was detected the mission had been completed. Of course, I'm not advocating that you do anything illegal or out of good character, but merely sharing my own experience.

One experience in particular proved to be quite the adventure. My group, the Family Tree and our record company, Kemetic Records were in Queen City (Charlotte, NC) promoting either the Paranormal Activity or Dark Ages II release, I'm not sure which one. In any event, we went to one of the local malls and started distributing flyers and selling our CDs. This was a new approach for selling CDs in the Charlotte area, so folks were intrigued and very supportive. It did not take long before mall security and local law enforcement were planning a course of action.

Being the vets that we are, the Family Tree and Kemetic Records Foot Soldiers were well aware of the developments. However, this only motivated us to increase our hand-to-hand sales in a most expedient (fast) manner. We were on the second level when mall security, backed by local law enforcement, approached us. Before they began to speak to us, we asked for their support in purchasing our new release. This caught security off guard and bought us a few more minutes to sell more CDs to people standing around who wanted to know what was going on. Eventually, security escorted us out of the mall, so we went to a few more malls a repeated the process. By the end of the day, we had accomplished our task, given the number of CDs we sold and the amount of flyers that were distributed.

The cost of printing flyers has become very economical over the years. Most printers make their money from design charges, so make sure that you know what you want or you could be paying a pretty penny for your design work. You might find a high school or college student that would design your artwork for exposure sake, versus receiving financial compensation. Let people around you know that you are looking for a graphic designer and you will come across someone that may assist you.

One of the ways that I have been able to consistently reach a larger demographic and reduce printing cost is by doing a "50/50" with other companies. Essentially, what happens is I find another company that will compliment my own and that is as eager as I am (if not more) to grind (promote). The company and I split the printing cost and we are both responsible for distributing the flyers. You might use this technique with other businesses to expand your own reach. This has proven to be very effective and a win/win for all parties involved. When using the printing companies below tell them JaWar, author of the *How to Self-Publish for Profit Book* sent you!

- Claxton Printing Co.
  408 Woodward Ave., SE, Atlanta, GA 30312
  P) 404-521-0933 F) 404-688-5446
  www.claxtonprinting.com
  jim@claxtonprinting.com

- Digiprint
  2395 Pleasantdale Rd., Suite 4-B, Atlanta, GA 30340
  P) 770-368-2060 F) 770-368-9943

- Envision Printing
  1266 Kennestone Cir, Suite 105, Marietta, GA 30066
  P) 678-355-6748 F) 404-355-6637
  www.envisionprinting.com
  cs@envisionprinting.com

- Extreme Media
  1440 Dutch Valley Pl., Suite 160
  P) 404-815-0553 F) 404-815-0314
  www.extremeatlanta.com

- Gazelle Printing & Consulting
  20 Executive Park Dr., Ste 2002, Atlanta, GA 30329
  P) 404-320-6926 Cell) 404-454-0668 F) 404-320-5450
  www.gazelleprinting.com
  dalegriffin@gazelleprinting.com

- Image Link
  1379 Chattahoochee Ave., Atlanta, GA 30318
  P) 404-605-0400 F) 404-605-0464
  www.imagelink.net
  staff2@imagelink.net

- Industry Outlet
  684 Antone St. Suite 105, Atlanta, GA 30318
  P) 404-417-9777 P) 877-417-9777 F) 404-759-2072
  print@theindustryoutlet.com

- Inkling Print and Design
  2483 E Briarcliff Rd., Atlanta, GA 30329
  P) 678-388-9662 F) 404-759-2154
  www.inklingprint.com
  info@inklingprint.com

- Kudzu Graphics
  1835 MacArthur Blvd., Atlanta, GA 30318
  P) 404-350-9776 F) 404-684-9554
  www.kudzugraphics.com

- Small Business Promotions, Inc.
  P.O. Box 1348, Lithonia, GA 30058
  P) 678-886-8792 P) 770-557-0938
  www.designsnprint.com
  orders@designsnprint.com

- Southern Poster Printing
  3862 Stevens Ct., Tucker, GA
  P) 888-872-8194 P) 404-872-8194

- Southern Stamp & Stencil
  428 Edgewood Ave., Atlanta, GA 30312
  P) 800-241-0985 P) 404-522-4431
  www.southernstamp.com
  info@southernstamp.com

WEBSITES THAT SELL DOMAIN NAMES

There is no excuse for not having a website if you are serious about building a successful career as an author or book publisher. A website should be included in your business, marketing and strategic plans. A few steps toward creating an on-line presence includes creating a domain (website) name that is easy to remember, relates to you or your business and registering that domain name.

There are a number of sites that allow you to create an on-line presence through their domain. While this should be utilized, at the end of the day you will want, and need to have, your own website address, such as **www.gojawar.com**, makemoneyselfpublishing.com, gomusicconnection.com or musicbusinessqanda.com. Having your own website address truly gives you your space on the internet. By owning and controlling your own site name, you may also decide to add additional revenue streams to your bottom line by selling advertising on your site. Below are a few sites where you may register your domain name. Keep in mind this is a very short list of companies that may register your domain name. Simply type "domain" or "website registration" in your favorite search and you will find a list of companies that provide similar services. Asking for references from family, friends and co-workers about companies that register website addresses may also yield great results. Remember a closed mouth does not get fed.

- www.buydomains.com
- www.networksolutions.com
- www.omnis.com
- www.yahoo.com

PHOTOGRAPHERS

- Arial Productions
  5115 Spring Creek LN., Dunwoody, GA 303050
  P) 770-394-9392

- D&G Enterprise
  P.O. Box 49692, Atlanta, GA 30359
  P) 678-755-0618 F) 404-633-6825
  www.dandgenterprise.biz

- DanmcCain Productions
  4459 Hwy 120, Duluth, GA 30097
  P) 770-853-2909
  www.danmccainproductions.com

- D2K Models Design Group
  1016 Howell Mill Rd., Suite 1210, Atlanta, GA 30318
  P) 404-441-5794
  www.d2kmodels.com
  moussa@d2kmodels.com

- Foto Illusion Studios
  2275 Northwest Parkway, Suite 115 Marietta, GA 30067
  P) 678-990-5211
  www.fotoillusion.com

- JWJ Photography
  2975 Headland Dr., Atlanta, GA 30331
  P) 404-783-0041

- Kenny's Photography
  1729 Rogers Ave. SW, Atlanta, GA 30310
  P) 404-758-7301 Cell) 404-247-2018

- Laser Photographics
  290 Hilderbrand Dr., Suite B-9, Atlanta, GA 30328
  P) 404-531-0555 F) 404-531-0044
  www.laserphotographics.com
  laserphotgraphics@mindsping.com

- Photomax
  3375 Buford Hwy, Suite 1020, Atlanta, GA 30329
  P) 404-320-1494 F) 404-320-6291
  www.photomax1hr.com
  photomax@aol.com

- Primetime
  P.O. Box 49531, Atlanta, GA 30359
  P) 404-731-2343
  www.primetimeatlanta.com

- Raw Talent Entertainment
  2900 Delk Rd., Suite 700 #133, Marietta, GA 30067

67

P) 404-207-0670
Raw_talent_ent@yahoo.com

- Sean Cokes Photography
  650 Hamilton Ave., Studio Z, Atlanta, GA 30312
  P) 404-622-7733
  www.seancokes.com
  scokesphoto@yahoo.com

- Tshanti Photography Studio
  300 MLK Jr. Dr., SE #144, Atlanta, GA 30312
  P) 678-768-4647
  tshantphoto@hotmail.com

MASTERING FACILITIES

Mastering is the art of fine-tuning an already fantastic reading that has been properly mixed. Before you say that your audio CD recording is complete- have you had it mastered by a mastering engineer? The mastering engineer should have years of experience and be familiar with mastering an audio book. Mastering an audio book is a technical science that normally requires years of experience by an educated professional.

Give your project a leg up over other audio books by having it professionally mastered by a mastering engineer. Like other professionals on your team you should interview the mastering engineer and ask for references of past and current clients. Below is a list of mastering engineers. Tell them you found them in the *How to Self-Publish for Profit* by JaWar.

- ➢ Aucourant Records
  P.O. Box 2231, Roswell, GA 30077

P) 770-640-9714
www.aucourantrecords.com
aucourant@aucourantrecords.com

➢ Atlanta Digital Mastering
Premier Plaza, 194 Jonesboro Rd., Suite O-3
Jonesboro, GA 30236
P) 678-698-2301

➢ Digitak Mastering
3603 MLK Blvd., Brunswick, GA 31520
P) 912-264-8673

➢ Fulton Post Works
3195 Buford Hwy., Suite 8, Duluth, GA 30096
P) 770-476-4915
www.fultonpostworks.com
jfulton@fultonpostworks.com

➢ Glenn Schick Mastering
3264 Shallowford Rd., Atlanta, GA 30341
P) 770-451-1314 F) 770-457-5243
www.gsmastering.com
gsmastering@earthlink.net

➢ Griffin Mastering
1051 Woodland Ave, Atlanta, GA 30316
P) 404-622-5102
www.mindspring.com/~gminc/
gminc@mindspring.com

➢ Pigpen Studios
101 Surry Ct., Athens, GA 30606
P) 706-369-6755
www.pigpenstudios.net
Daniel@pigpenstudios.net

• Sonare Recordings

309 Gloucester Rd., Savannah, GA 31410
P) 912-484-8451
www.sonarerecordings.com

- Wave Guide Studios
2062 Weems Road, Atlanta, GA 30084
P) 770-939-2004 F) 770-938-4840
www.waveguidestudios.com
info@waveguidestudios.com

- Wizzard Media
3500 Lenox Rd., Suite 1500, Atlanta, GA 30326
P) 404-321-3201 P) 800-352-8390 F) 404-633-0940
www.moneygrow.com/wizzard
wizard@moneygrow.com

TEN WAYS TO MAKE MONEY FROM YOUR BOOK

PAPERBACK & HARDBACK BOOKS

Your first source of revenue as a self-published author will be through selling the print version of your books. The print version of your book may be sold in chain bookstores like Barnes & Noble, Borders and Books-A-Million, independent bookstores and specialty stores and shops. For example, my book *The Atlanta Music Industry Connection* is sold in many local record stores. It's kind of funny when I think of initially selling the book to record stores. For me it was a "no brainer", but record store owners and managers didn't think the book was going to sell very well in their stores. I knew that music industry professionals were often in certain record stores and that once they saw the book they would buy it. My hunch was right. I had stores screaming at me because I had not restocked the store with more books after they sold out. Follow your hunch, gut feeling, third eye, God Force, instinct, whatever you call it and act on it with practical planning and precision.

More of your sales may end up coming from non-bookstores. If you consider that there are more other type of stores then there are bookstores, then you will open yourself up to a larger market. If your book will sell in a store; the store will be happy to have your book, especially if you are a professional and deal like a businessperson who has authored a book versus an author who is in business. Seek out stores that draw upon your target market and get your book into those stores.

Many non-bookstores may be reluctant to carry your book. However, if you make the process painless, systematic and a no lose opportunity for them you greatly increase the chance of being able to sell your book in their store. Before going in, make sure that you have your needed consignment forms, receipt book, business cards, promotional materials like flyers and bookmarks, a small bookstand and your books. This will demonstrate that you are a professional and gives the illusion that you have done this many times before even if you have not. If you are a shy person you will need to get over that immediately. You can do this by practicing how and what you will say in front of the mirror and in front of others. You may get consignment forms from your local business supply store or by doing a search on the internet. I would simply type "consignment forms" in your favorite search engine. Look at all the forms that you have and use the one that best fits your needs or you may take the best from all of them and create your own agreement.

In addition, to making the process painless and systematic for non-bookstore owners, you will want to ensure them that it is only a no lose opportunity for them. As an example you should not ask the store to buy your books from you outright when initially attempting to put your book in the store. When your books begin to sell you may offer your books at a greater discount if the store buys the books from you upfront. Your first source of revenue as a self-published author will be through selling the print version of your books. Having your books sold in stores will increase your credibility as an author and publisher. As you read throughout this section you will find that this is only the tip of the iceberg from which you may generate additional profits from your book. My company provides book-printing services. Get started today call 1-800-963-0949 or 678-887-4656.

E-BOOKS

The second source of revenue from your existing book will be through e-books. "E-books" simply means electronic books. E-books allow for readers to buy the book over the internet in electronic form. E-books may be downloaded to personal data assistance devices (like blackberry phones) for those people always on the go. They are great, because there is little to no additional cost associated with selling them once your original book has been created. With an e-book you'll want to consider ease of download from your website, payment method and security. In addition to selling your e-book on your site you will need to encourage others to help you promote and sell your book. You can do this by creating an affiliate (referral) system. The great thing about an affiliate (referral) system is that you only pay when a product is sold through another website. The person who has the affiliate website does not have to do much. There is a financial incentive for them to draw visitors to your site to buy your e-book. It is a win/win scenario. All e-books that I have seen have been in a PDF Format. PDF is a compression application. What that means is you would take your book that is already in a word document an convert it to a PDF file. When you convert your book to a PDF it is compressed making it smaller in size and allowing it to be easily sent via email. In addition to compression, the PDF is like taking a digital picture of each page of your book.

Paypal is probably the most well-known and accepted payment method used by buyers and sellers on the internet. You can visit paypal.com to get details on how to start accepting paypal on your website. In addition, to Paypal, you will want to take major credit cards on your site. In order to accept credit cards, you will need to either set up a merchant account or outsource the service through another company.

Security is a feature you will need to employ when selling your e-book. You will need security for payment method and security to ensure that your book is not easily bootlegged. Download the step-by-step system on how to make money self publishing at **makemoneyselfpublishing.com**. The system is the same one I used to create a sell my first ebooks. I continue to use the same system today. In fact, the Make Money Self Publishing Kit was used to create **makemoneyselfpublishing.com**. You can use the information you download at **makemoneyselfpublishing.com** over and over to create an unlimited amount of ebooks, special reports and info-products that will position you to make residual/passive income virtually forever.

AUDIO BOOKS

The third source of revenue from your existing book will be through audio books. Audio books are real cool because people can listen to your book while on the move. They may listen to your audio book in the car, on the plane, train or boat, while standing still or on the go. They may hear it while at the neighborhood coffee house or bookstore. One of the best parts about having an audio book is the ability to easily capture new fans, listeners and readers of your print version. If the driver of a car is listening to your audio book and has passengers then the passengers are subject to it hear as well. Likewise, college professors or high school teachers may decide to use your audio book as an instructional tool during class. There are a number of applications where a group of people may listen to your audio book at the same time.

On the surface this may sound like a bad thing because everyone has not bought your product. After awhile some of the folks will buy your audio or print book, because they can't stand not having their own. I view this as paid promotion. Someone paid to promote you, meaning they bought your book and our now promoting you by letting others listen to your message or story in audio book form. Trust me- it could be far worse, they could not tell a soul and never listen to your audio book again. The other advantage of having more people listen to your audio book is you continue to build your brand. The more that people hear your name, read your book or listen to your voice the greater your brand becomes. If your book is an informational or how to guide it will increase your credibility as a professional and expert in your field. As a self-published author you may not have an extensive marketing budget, or the depth of contacts that a major publishing house does. On the other hand, you have greater creative control over your marketing dollars and efforts. Your audio book may prove to be a great additional revenue stream.

RECORDING STUDIOS

As an author you should determine the goal, create a practical plan and rehearse the plan before paying studio costs to record. This will save a great deal of time and money.

There is a wide range of studios at your disposal. When it comes to recording, a good rule of thumb is the fewer the surprises, the better off you are. With that in mind, one of the questions you will want to ask is if the quoted price includes the studio engineer's fee, as sometimes it does and sometimes it doesn't, so remember to ask. In addition, many studios offer block (discount) rates when you book (reserve) say 10 or more hours at a time. Therefore, it is to your advantage to block out studio time to save money. However, if you are not accustomed to recording for 10 hours then this may be a waste of time and money. Studio prices may range from $35/hr to $200/hr.

Remember to bring your own CD-Rs and other record-able devices to the studio. The studio will probably have some on hand, but it will cost you a lot more money to buy it from the studio rather than to bring your own. Remember, the recording studio is in business to make a profit, so they are going to make every penny they can. In addition to studio cost, you want to ask about the experience of the studio engineer that will work on your project and if they have experience recording audio-books.

In summary, a few factors to consider before choosing a recording studio are: studio cost, experience of studio engineer and chemistry between you and the engineer. You may find studios in any part of the country by looking in the phone book, visiting music equipment stores that sell instruments and record stores and asking the staff about local studios in the area. Typing in your city and "recording studios" (e.g. Salt Lake City Recording Studios) in your favorite search engine should help you find studios. Asking local musicians, band teachers at high schools and colleges should also help you find studios. Once you start asking- the answers will come. Below is a list of recording studios in the Atlanta area. By using the tools and resources mentioned above you should be able to locate studios in your city. When contacting the recording studios below let them know that you found them in the *How to Self-Publish for Profit Book* by JaWar.

- 2201 Studios
  2459 Roosevelt Hwy, Ste. C-5, College Park, GA 30337
  P) 404-762-5744
  www.2201studios.com
  info@2201studios.com

- 2 High Recording Studios
  540 Permalume Place, Atlanta, GA 30318
  P) 404-603-9771 F) 404-475-0618
  www.2highstudios.com
  info@2highstudios.com

- 2ND 2 Nunn Recording Studio
  1558 North Highway 27, Carrollton, GA 30117
  P) 770-214-1707 P) 866-208-3505
  www.2nd2nunn.com
  studio@2nd2nunn.com

- 302 Entertainment
  850 Marcus Hyah Ct., Atlanta, GA 30349
  P) 770-909-7202

- 4th Generation Productions
  3140 Mangum Ln., SW, Atlanta, GA 30311
  P) 404-691-6493
  www.105entertainment.com
  jimmyswagger@hotmail.com

- 500 Grand Studios
  Contact: Carlos Foreman
  1850 Graves Rd., Suite 215, Norcross, GA 30093
  P) 770-985-8354

- ACA Digital Recording, Inc.
  P.O. Box 450727, Atlanta, GA 31145
  P) 404-284-0948 F) 404-284-7429

- Air Tyte Recordings
  312 Collier Rd., Barnesville, GA 31145
  P) 770-358-7552

- All Good Productions
  120 Interstate Pkwy., Suite 164, Atlanta, GA 30339
  P) 770-956-9698 P) 877-294-0863
  www.allgood.net

- APC Recording Studios
  3838 Oakcliff Industrial Court, Atlanta, GA 30340
  P) 770-242-7678
  www.apcstudios.com
  stuff@apcstudios.com

- Arcadia Recording Studio
  4540-B South Berkeley Lake Road, Norcross, GA 30071
  P) 770-448-9992
  www.arcadiarocks.com
  info@arcadiarocks.com

- Big Cat Studios
  500 Bishop St., Suite E5, Atlanta, GA 30318

P) 404-603-8229 P) 404-438-7371

- Bizzi Beats Studios
  3274 E. Main St., College Park, GA 30337
  P) 404-259-4352
  www.bizzibeats.com
  sta_bizzibnt@hotmail.com

- Blackberry Recordings
  3141 E. Ponce DeLeon Ave., Scottdale, GA 30079
  P) 678-361-0692
  blackberrysounds@aol.com

- Blue Sound Studios
  P.O. Box 191141, Atlanta, GA 31119-1141
  P) 404.327.4228 P) 877.327.4228 F) 404.327.7769
  www.bluesoundstudios.com
  info@bluesoundstudios.com
- Blue Studio Productions
  4925 Lakeside Dr., Atlanta, GA 30360
  P) 770-451-3007
  www.thebluestudio.com
  office@thebluestudio.com

- Caber Media
  126 N. Peachtree St., Norcross, GA 30071
  P) 404-520-5055
  www.cabermedia.com
  info@cabermedia.com

- Captive Sound Recording Studio
  1442 Tullie Rd NE, Atlanta, GA 30329
  P) 404-325-4860
  www.captivesound.com

- Catspaw Productions
  922 Curie Drive, Alpharetta, GA 30005
  P) 678-624-7660 P) 888-807-2639 F) 678-624-7557

www.catspawproductions.com
info@catspawproductions.com

- Cherry Recording Studios
  800 East Ave NE, Atlanta, GA 30312
  P) 404-524-7757

- Claymore Studios
  2459 Roosevelt Highway, Suite B-16
  College Park, GA 30337
  P) 404-762-5021 F) 404-762-5524
  www.landmine-ent.com

- CMO Studio
  2310-D Marietta Blvd., Atlanta, GA 30318
  P) 404-355-0909 F) 404-352-2136
  www.cmopro.com
  cmopro@cmopro.com

- Creative Sound Concepts
  1495 Northside Dr., Suite D, Atlanta, GA 30318
  P) 404-873-6628 F) 404-367-9599
  creativesound@mindspring.com

- DMC Productions
  P.O. Box 2253, Stockbridge, GA 30281
  P) 404-931-4373 P) 404-964-7026 F) 734-448-2968
  www.dmcpro.net

- Doppler Recording Studios
  1922 Piedmont Circle, Atlanta, GA 30324
  P) 404-873-6941 F) 404-249-7148
  www.dopplerstudios.com
  info@dopplerstudios.com

- Earcandy Recording
  204 W. Poplar St., Suite A, Griffin, GA 30224
  P) 770-228-2066

www.earcandyrecording.com

- Elaborate Productions Inc.
  6020 Dawson Boulevard, Suite D, Norcross, GA 30093
  P) 770-447-4427 F) 770-447-4428
  www.elaborateproductions.com
  mixmonstersinc@bellsouth.net

- Electronika Recording Studios
  2963 Stone Road, Atlanta, GA 30344
  P) 404-766-0288

- Exocet Recording Studios
  3264 Shallowford Rd, Chamblee, GA 30341
  P) 770-455-7256 F) 770-457-5243
  www.exocetstudios.com
  info@exocetstudios.com

- Gabriel Studios
  6920 Jimmy Carter Blvd., Suite 200
  Norcross, GA 30071
  P) 770-409-0333
  www.gabrielstudios.com
  barry@gabrielstudios.com

- Gibson Recording
  595 Huntwick Pl., Roswell, GA 30075
  P) 770-518-0404 F) 404-843-4334

- Gold Cast Recording
  485 West Crossville Rd., Roswell, GA 30075
  P) 678-886-3353

- Go-Town Studios
  2093 Faulkner Rd., NE, Atlanta, GA 30324
  P) 404-325-0882 F) 404-325-0196
  www.cash-awn.com
- Group Effort Studios

842 Marietta St., Atlanta, GA 30318
P) 770-633-0050
www.groupeffortstudios.com
booking@groupeffortstudios.com

- House 21 Entertainment Recording Studio
  2100 Drake Court, Lithonia, GA 30058
  P) 678-508-3742

- JFX Studio
  1823 Tree Top Way, Marietta, GA 30062
  P) 770-977-0982
  www.jfxstudio.com

- Joi Recording Studios
  2356 Park Central Blvd., Decatur, GA 30035
  P) 678-418-9973

- Kashmere Studios
  1200 Spring St., Atlanta, GA 30309
  P) 404-379-7126
  www.kashmerestudios.com
  russ@kashmerestudios.com

- LedBelly Sound Studio
  P.O. Box 2202, Woodstock, Georgia 30188
  P) 770-345-0908 F) 770-345-9639
  www.ledbellysound.com
  Matt@LedBellySound.com

- Lighthouse
  2966 Winn Drive, Lawrenceville, GA 30044
  P) 770-381-7106
  http://members.aol.com/lhsestudio

- Mayday Sound Studio
  3875 Green Industrial Way, #600, Chamblee, GA 30341
  P) 770-457-5551

maydaysound@earthlink.net

- Maze Recording Studio
  2963 Lambert Dr., Atlanta, GA 30324
  Cell) 770-633-5747 P) 678-428-3437

- McMix
  2878 Jonquil Dr., Smyrna, GA 30080
  P) 770-436-9620
  www.mcmix.com
  mcmix@mcmix.com

- Media Expressions
  525 Emerald Lake Path, Sugar Hill, GA 30518
  P) 678-462-6083 F) 678-482-7980
  www.thormusic.com
  info@thormusic.com

- Mega Mix Studios
  101 Kenwood Rd., Suite 38, Fayetteville, GA
  P) 770-255-8538 P) 770-461-0050
  www.georgiamediagroup.com

- Morrow House Studios
  251 Bighton Way, Marietta, GA 30066
  P) 770-422-3859
  www.morrowhousestudios.com
  max@morrowhousestudios.com

- National Recording Corporation
  P.O.Box 5111, Rome, GA 30162
  P) 706-234-4864
  www.narecorp.com
  info@narecorp.com

- Nickel & Dime Recording Studios
  106 N. Avondale Rd., Avondale Estates, GA 30002
  www.nickelanddimestudios.net

P) 404-297-0955

- Night Sky Music
  223 Manley Rd., Griffin, GA 30223
  P) 770-229-5554
  www.nightskymusicstudio.com

- Oasis Recording Studio
  750 Ralph McGill Blvd., Atlanta, Georgia 30312
  P) 404-525-4440 F) 404-525-4545
  www.oasisrecording.com
  info@oasisrecording.com

- One Star Recording
  5724 Riverdale Rd., Suite C-4, College Park, GA 30349
  P) 678-791-9607

- Orphan Studio
  684 Antone Street, Suite 110, Atlanta, Georgia 30318
  P) 404-352-0666 F) 404-351-7775
  www.orphanstudio.com
  glenn@orphanstudio.com

- Out Da Cutt
  2964 Ember Dr., Suite 207, Decatur, GA 30032
  P) 678-508-2318

- P. Mazo Sound Company
  4 Mall Court, Savannah, GA 31406
  P) 706-354-6006 F) 706-354-3682
  www.pmazosound.com
  paul@pmazound.com

- Paradise Recording Studio
  1651 Link Overlook, Atlanta, GA 30088
  P) 404-351-0086

- Patchwerk Recording Studios

1094 Hemphill, Atlanta, GA 30318
P) 404-874-9880

- PB Recording Studio
  605 Suite-C Moultrie Road, Albany, GA 31705
  P) 229-349-0019

- Platinum Sound Recording Studio
  500-A N. Slappery Blvd., Albany, GA 31701
  P) 229-883-3009

- Playground Recording Studios
  636 Exchange Pl, Suite 100, Lilburn, GA 30045
  P) 770-921-6611 F) 678-924-0335
  damonttoure@aol.com

- Power Source Entertainment
  5295 Highway 78, Suite D-359
  Stone Mountain, GA 30087
  P) 404-288-3638 Cell) 404-886-8105
  www.powersource-ent.com

- Pro South Entertainment Recording Studios
  3060 Bugle Dr., Duluth, GA 30096
  P) 770-455-3828 F) 770-455-3821
  www.prosouthentertainment.com
  info@prosouthentertainment.com

- Red Swan Studio
  5658 Riverdale Rd., Unit-Q, College Park, GA 30349
  P) 770-909-9779

- Rex Trax Inc.
  1255 Buford Hwy., Suite 206, Suwanee, GA 30024
  P) 678-730-0008 F) 678.868.1247
  www.rextrax.com
  service@rextrax.com

- Rockstudio
  1409 Newcastle St., Brunswick, GA 31520
  www.rockstudio.com
  info@rockstudio.com
  P) 912 280-0227

- Shangri-La Recordings
  1456 Boulevard SE, Atlanta, GA 30315
  P) 404-624-4092 F) 404-624-4045
  www.shangri-lastudios.com
  music@shangri-lastudios.com

- Signal Flow Entertainment Inc.
  775 North Ave. #261, Jonesboro, GA 30226
  P) 770-994-9580
  www.signalflowent.com

- Silent Sound Studios
  588 Trabert Ave., Atlanta, GA 30309
  P) 404-350-9199 F) 404-350-9562

- Sonica
  500 Bishop Street, Suite C-2, Atlanta, GA 30318
  P) 404-350-9540 F) 404-350-9439
  www.sonicarecording.com
  john@sonicarecording.com steve@sonicarecording.com

- Sound Decision Studios
  P.O. Box 4141, Duluth, GA 30096
  P) 770-813-1870
  www.sounddecisionstudios.com
  bstephens@sounddecisionstudios.com

- Sound Level Recording
  6181 Memorial Drive #A, Stone Mountain, GA 30083
  P) 770-469-2021
  www.soundlevelstudio.com

info@soundlevelstudio.com

- Sound Master Recording Studio
  P.O. Box K, Alma, GA, 31510
  P) 912-632-0244 F) 912-632-0703
  www.soundmasterstudio.com

- Southern Tracks Recording
  3051 Clairmont Rd., NE, Atlanta, GA 30329
  P) 404-329-0147 F) 404-329-0162
  www.southerntracks.com
  mike@southerntracks.com

- Street Gospel Recording Studio
  6595-G Roswell Road, Suite 689, Atlanta, GA 30328
  P) 404-512-6296 P) 404-222-2474 F) 404-223-5306
  jasonmills@tmail.com

- Studio A
  3193 Lawrenceville Hwy, Tucker, GA 30383
  P) 770-491-3928

- Syncrecy Recordings
  P.O. Box 742, Atlanta, GA 30019
  P) 678-377-8892
  www.syncrecy.com
  syncrecy@aol.com

- The A Room Recording Studio
  255 Bottley Dr., Suite 54, Atlanta, GA 30324
  P) 404-249-7166 F) 404-249-7338
  www.thearoom.net
  info@thearoom.net

- The Muzic Lab Recording Studio
  5222 North Henry Blvd., Ste-K Stockbridge, GA 30281
  P) 678-565-1616
  www.taecusa.com

info@taecusa.com

- The Odyssey Studio
  198 N. First Street, Colbert, GA 30628
  P) 706-540-1076
  www.theodysseystudio.com
  P_Rives@TheOdysseyStudio.com

- The Sound Lab
  2652 S. Cobb Dr., Suite C, Smyrna, GA 30080
  P) 770-803-0014 F) 770-803-9198 Cell) 678-520-5373
  www.soundlabstudio.com
  info@soundlabstudio.com or thesoundlab@earthlink.net

- Trac City Entertainment
  Greenbriar Marketplace
  2975 Headland Dr., Booth D-6, Atlanta, GA 30311
  P) 678-904-7905 Cell) 770-256-5409

- Tree Sound Studios
  4610 Peachtree Industrial Blvd., Norcross GA 30071
  P) 770-242-8944 F) 770-242-0155
  www.treesoundstudios.com
  nina@treesoundstudios.com

- Twelve Oak Studios
  620 Powder Springs St., Smyrna, GA 30080
  P) 770-435-2220

- Upper Room Studios
  403 Reagan Rd., Rebecca, GA 31783
  P) 229-831-7585
  www.upperroomrecording.com
  greg@upperroomrecording.com

- Venusian Music Studio
  P.O. Box 46502, Lawrenceville, GA 30044
  P) 404-840-7574

www.venusianmusicstudio.com
info@vnusianmusicstudio.com

- VMG Studios- Vision Music Group, Inc.
  1360 Union Hill Rd Suite 3-H. Alpharetta, GA 30004
  P) 770-754-4543 F) 770-754-0404
  www.vmgstudio.com

- Wet Basement Studios
  225 Corinth Ct., Roswell, GA 30075
  P) 770-993-8074 F) 770-993-4961
  www.wetbasement.com
  lynn@wetbasement.com

- Whippoorwill Sound
  2878 Jonquil Drive, Smyrna, Georgia 30080
  P) 770-333-9372
  www.atlantastudio.com
  wilhodge@mindspring.com

- White Dog Studios
  800 Forrest St. N.W. Atlanta GA 30318
  P) 404-355-2200 F) 404-355-2204
  www.whitedogstudios.net
  info@whitedogstudios.net

- Wonder Dog Sounds
  920 Roxton Cir., Marietta, GA 30064
  P) 770-693-3954
  www.wonderdogsounds.com

- Writeside Productions
  327 Buckingham Drive, Marietta GA 30066
  P) 770-928-1955
  www.writeside.biz
  david@writeside.biz

- ZAC-Zumpano Recording Complex

669 Antone Street NW, Atlanta, GA 30318
P) 404-603-8040 F) 404-603-8010
www.zacrecording.com
info@zacrecording.com

CD and DVD MANUFACTURERS

You will need to consider set-up prices, over & under run charges, turnaround time, taxes, shipping/handling and hidden cost before getting your CD or Vinyl pressed.

Set-up prices vary from company to company and project to project, but normally are associated with any first printing project. For instance, there was a set-up cost of like $100 for a CD release I had several years ago. After your first printing there usually is no more set-up fees. Of course, if you change something on the CD or insert anything, then you will be subject to a new set-up fee.

To ensure that the price you are quoted is the price that you pay for duplication, always ask at the end of your conversation with the manufacturer "Are there any other fees that I need to be aware of? For example, does the price you just quoted me include taxes, shipping/handling and/or any other fees that I may not be aware of?" This will ensure you pay the price you are quoted and not a penny more.

There are a number of factors to consider when selecting what company should manufacturer your CD or DVD. These factors will vary based on your need. However, customer service, competitive pricing, quality control, turn around time and industry support are a few reasons you should consider choosing one of the manufacturers below.

Any company you select should provide you with superior customer service. Superior customer service is a staff that is friendly, knowledgeable, quick to return your phone calls and emails and meets or exceeds your expectations. A friendly and knowledgeable staff is one that always greets you in a professional and warm manner and seems to answer all your questions concerning manufacturing your product. The music industry is moving faster and faster as the digital age continues to dictate the process of recording, marketing, distribution and collection of royalties of our music. Your manufacturer should be able to respond to your inquiries within a reasonable time frame. "Reasonable" will be defined by how quickly companies' competitors respond, by the companies' response rate policy, (for example, some companies say they will return all phone calls within 24 to 48 hours) and how soon you think they should respond. Through every aspect of the manufacturing process the company you select should meet or exceed your expectations.

Most of the companies below will charge about the same price to manufacturer CD's and DVD's. If you find that prices vary greatly between one company and the next you will want to consider two questions. First, you will want to ask yourself why there are major differences in the pricing between companies. If you find that all things are equal (meaning you are comparing "apples to apples") then you will want to ask the company with the higher price if they match local competitors' prices. Typically, companies will price match advertised prices if they are able to. What I mean is some companies by blank CD's in bulk numbers. Because they do so, they are able to get them at substantially lower prices than competitors. They can pass along the savings to their customers. But some companies purchase blank CD's at higher prices and they simply cannot price match competitors; but beware- all that seems equal between companies may not be. Listen very carefully when talking to a manufacturer to ensure you fully *over*stand what they are saying.

The company or companies you do business with should have some form of QC or Quality Control. Quality control ensures that your product will be made at the highest standard possible to give you the competitive edge in the marketplace. It will ensure you compete on a major scale. Larger manufacturers tend to have the best quality control, but at the very minimum any manufacturer should be willing to replace or refund you for any product that was not made properly if it was there fault. However, if your recording had a blemish during the recording process this is your issue, as this should have been fixed during recording and mastering not the manufacturing process. You should always strive to obtain the highest quality possible and so should the people you do business with.

Turn around time is extremely important, especially if you have a show or release party planned and expect to have your music back in a reasonable time frame. Remember to always ask when your product will be complete and the company's policy if the product is not ready by that time. Be sure to ask the difference between your product being complete and your product being available to be shipped or picked up. The completion date seldom is the date you will have your product back. For instance, if you order your DVD's on March 5 and the company says that they will be ready on March 10, that may mean the duplication or replication will be complete by March 10 and they will be ready to pick up from the office on March 11 or they will shipped on March 11. If you can pick them up on March 11 then great, but if they have to be shipped to you then it may take anywhere from one to five days before you will actually have your DVD's. If it took five days to ship you wouldn't have your product back until March 15- this definitely is not March 10, although your product was ready on March 10. I mentioned all this because many times there is miscommunication between the manufacturing company and the client and this can lead to many delays and frustration on both sides of the table. Follow this information and you should be ok. Once you get the answer to the questions above always ask to have them put it in writing, no matter what. I don't care if your mama, brother or sister is manufacturing the CD's or DVD's- get in writing.

There are a number of factors to consider when selecting what company should manufacturer your CD or DVD. These factors will vary based on your need. The company should provide superior customer service, offer competitive pricing, maintain quality control and have a quick turn around time. The *Los Angeles Music Industry Connection and Atlanta Music Industry Connection Books* have a list of companies that make CDs and DVDs. You may download these books at **gomusicconnection.com**.

> Creative Media
> 2783 Senecca Trail, Duluth, GA 30096-6298

P) 770-447-8137
www.creativemedia.com
sales@creativemedia.com

➢ Da Real Hometeam
P.O. Box 1973, Atlanta, GA 30301
P) 678-508-9274
www.darealhometeam.com
info@darealhometeam.com

➢ HT Media
P.O. Box 1295, Lithonia, GA 30058
P) 770-987-9200 F) 770-987-2385

➢ Mindzai
1139 Euclid Avenue, Atlanta, GA 30307
P) 404-577-8484 F) 404-577-5895
www.mindzai.net

➢ ON4 Productions
684 Antone St., NW Suite 110, Atlanta, GA 30318
P) 888-710-5157 P) 404-603-9900 F) 404-351-7775
www.on4prod.com

➢ Project 70 Audio Services
433 Bishop St., NW Suite CD, Atlanta, GA 30310
P) 404-875-7000 F) 404-875-7007
www.project70.com

➢ Straight from the Soul
5741 Wells Circle, Stone Mountain, GA 30087
P) 770-413-2464
straightent@aol.com

➢ Tape Warehouse
2688 Peachtree Sq., Doraville, GA 30360
P) 770-458-1679 F) 770-458-0276
www.tapewarehouse.com

MP3

The fourth source of revenue from your existing book will be through MP3's. With your audio books you will want to offer sections and chapters of your book as downloadable MP3's from your website. MP3 is a compression format for audio much like PDF is a compression format for word documents. MP3's allow for your audio books to quickly be sold and distributed through digital distribution. Most audio software pre-installed on computers allows you to easily convert your audio files to an MP3. The MP3's available for download will help you greatly increase your revenue stream.

Let's say that you had a book with fifteen chapters and the entire audio book sold for $20. You might sell each chapter as a digital download with a price point of anywhere from $1.99 to $5.99. At these prices- you have greatly increased your profit margin per chapter sold. You have made it affordable for people who may be willing to buy one or more chapters without paying the entire $20. However, they may find themselves coming back and buying the entire book. I would imagine this is great for technical or how to books. It is wonderful for novels where people may not want to spend the entire dollar amount without sampling a chapter or two.

Your price points will be determined by a number of factors. The most important being the price at which you are willing to sell your downloads and the price at which your buyers are willing to purchase. The happy medium between the two should be your actual retail price to your customers.

STREAMING AUDIO & INTERNET RADIO

The fifth source of revenue from your existing book will be through streaming audio and internet radio. What makes streaming audio and internet radio great is it could work for informative, interview and story telling formats. There are four ways that streaming audio and internet radio could help you generate additional revenue from your existing audio book. First, you could employ the "pay to play" format. With the pay to play format, listeners would simply go to your website, type in their credit card number or send money through Paypal over a secure server and have access to one or more of your audio streams. Second, you could charge a monthly membership fee to end users on your site and they could listen to your audio streams as much as they like as long as they were paying members. You would simply need to ensure that you continually offer and create new content. This should not be very difficult given that there is always someone with something to say. You could begin featuring lesser known and well-established authors and industry professionals during your audio broadcast. Third, you could charge sponsors or advertisers to be featured in your audio stream. This could work in three ways. You could either mention that this broadcast is brought to you by XYZ Company. You could mention the sponsors name at the end of the broadcast or you could mention the advertisers name while sharing your information. For example, if I had an audio stream speaking about questions to ask before going into a recording studio, I could easily charge a studio to mention there contact details in my discussion. Finally, you could make your audio stream free and increase the amount of traffic to your site where you could, in turn, justify charging advertisers to pay to have a presence on your site. I think this would be more of a secondary or an incentive based opportunity for advertisers who pay to be mentioned in your audio broadcast. The reason I say this is as society becomes increasingly mobile and are able to listen to satellite radio, more people will have access to audio streams and internet radio while in their daily routine, but may not always be in front of a computer screen to view ads. Essentially, as technology improves I imagine you will be able to reach more people through an audio broadcast.

Keep in mind that companies and individuals are currently employing the revenue models mentioned. However, you have what know one else has, you have you! Because you are selling your information as much as you are selling yourself, you'll want to concentrate heavily on building your brand. Your name should draw a certain demographic; likewise your information should draw a certain demographic. The goal is to continue to expand your reach. The more listeners and subscribers you have the greater your revenue generating potential. Case in point: Oprah Winfrey has millions of viewers, because she does, her show is able to generate massive profits from advertisers. Likewise she has parlayed her viewership into readership of her magazine O. The possibilities of additional revenue from streaming audio and internet radio are vast. The beauty is that you will already have much of your content created from your audio book.

You'll find additional resources on how to make money online at **gojawar.com**, **moneyonline.blogspot.com** and **moneygoldmine.blogspot.com**.

DVD BOOKS

The sixth source of revenue from your existing book will be through DVD Books. A DVD book may be organized in interview or infomercial formats. While this may work for technical and how to resource guides, it may not work well for novel or fantasy genres. However, a novel or fantasy book may be turned into a movie, which could be sold as a DVD. I will discuss this further in the next section. In addition, a DVD may work for children's books. I imagine you would need to be very creative, making the DVD interactive to ensure that you are retaining the child's attention while teaching them at the same time.

The great thing about creating a DVD book is it could be a bit more interactive than an audio book. It may justify you charging a higher retail price versus the print or audio versions. Because of the visual component you may reference the print version of your book by showing what it looks like. This should increase your profit margin. One of the cool things about creating a DVD book is you could use your existing channels of distribution to supply the market. That means you will sell the DVD at retail stores, on your website and in the back of the room when you do your speaking engagements.

Because there are additional pricing factors in creating a DVD including production, editing, manufacturing, marketing and promotions, you will want to conduct market research on your existing client base. "Test Before You Press" is a phrase often used in the music business. Basically, it means that you print a limited supply of product and give it to a select group to gauge their response- whether positive or negative. You ask them for ways to improve the product line. By carefully listening and implementing what appears to be a consensus you greatly improve your chances for success.

In ensuring that you get a professional look, feel and sound from your DVD book without investing huge amounts of money, you may want to secure college or high school talent. Most students are looking for ways to build their resume while tweaking their own creative juices. It is potentially a win/win opportunity, given that you include the students name and contact information at the end of DVD and/or in the associated packaging. Whenever someone asks the students for a sample of their work, they could give them a copy of your DVD. This also creates greater marketing opportunity for your product line.

When considering music for your DVD keep in mind that you must get permission from the copyright owner before including any music on your video. Hit songs will probably cost you more money and time than it is worth. I would suggest having a band, producer or musician create music for you or using music from an independent artist who would take a much smaller amount of money to license their work for use in your DVD. To ensure that you don't infringe upon any ones copyright, you will want to contact an entertainment attorney. I have a list of entertainment attorneys in the *Atlanta Music Industry Connection* and *Los Angeles Music Industry Connection Books.* You may complete and mail in the order form in the back of the book or visit **www.gojawar.com** or **gomusicconnection.com** to get your copy of either book.

MOVIES

Movies, documentaries, direct to video, T.V., cable, major and independent film releases are the seventh source of revenue from your existing book. Approaching these sources will most likely require agents, attorneys, business managers and a bit of being at the right place at the right time. In addition, to seeking to have your book turned into a feature film, cable or TV show, you may seek to go the independent route. This is not out of the realm of possibilities considering that you may have already self-published your book.

In addition, you may seek to turn your book into a documentary. There are a number of film festivals held throughout the year around the country. You might find an independent filmmaker willing to turn your vision into reality. This would give a filmmaker another opportunity to create a new film without having to write a script from scratch. To locate film festivals do a search in your favorite search engine by typing in any of the following: "independent film festival", "national film festivals", "United States film festivals" and so forth. This is a vast subject with a huge earning potential; I simply wanted to introduce the thought to you. Remember to consult an entertainment attorney before signing any agreements. You may find a list of entertainment attorneys in the *Atlanta Music Industry Connection* and *Los Angeles Music Industry Connection*. Either book may be downloaded as an ebook by visiting either **gojawar.com** or **gomusiconnection.com**.

PUBLIC SPEAKING

The eighth source of revenue from your existing book will be through speaking engagements. Through success of your book your notoriety will increase. As your name grows in popularity and you become more respected in your field. You may be sought after for speaking engagements. Initially, I would suggest speaking every chance you get. Remember you'll want to build your professional speaking portfolio as others have done. This is especially true if you don't have advance degrees. As you're requested more you, can choose which engagements to attend. While you want to get paid for speaking you will want to do some activities that are free of charge to share with people who are less fortunate and are unable to make a paid engagement or for those who are not familiar with whom you are. The amount of time you devote to these opportunities are totally up to you.

One of the most important things you will want to have is a rider contract. Essentially, a rider contract outlines the terms of your engagement. You will want to ensure there is a space in the back of the room for you to sign and sell your books. As a self-published author, or even one signed to a major publishing house, the majority of your initial sales will come from back room sells. You will want to video record all of your speaking engagements, as they may be used to improve future presentations. In addition, the videos may be edited and sold as DVDs, turned into documentaries or audio books.

MERCHANDISING & ENDORSEMENT DEALS

The ninth source of revenue from your existing book will be through merchandising rights. To ensure that you are able to take full advantage of merchandising rights you'll want to obtain a trademark for your name and/or logo. You may either secure a state or federal trademark. While a state trademark gives protection for the state that you are doing business in a federal trademark protects you in all of the United States. A state trademark normally is obtained through the secretary of state, while the federal trademark is obtained through the U.S. Patent and Trademark Office their number is 800-786-9199.

Merchandising allows you to generate additional money from your existing brand. In essence, you can either manufacture goods in house and/or license other companies to do it for you. Manufacturing goods in house means that you would be responsible for getting various items printed with your name, logo or catch phrase on them and bringing them to market. That would include a similar process to create your book. You would need to think of your intended audience, production cost, creative content, marketing, distribution and royalty collection. While this may sound a bit extensive, it is the same thing you would do for your book on a local, regional, national or international scale. The difference is your book would be the primary product line, whereas your merchandise would be secondary, growing in popularity in part because of your book. Merchandising your own product line is great as it allows you to learn and grow new business that could help make you rich. However, it is better to have a team of like-minded professionals to execute a plan.

With that being said, licensing your work would be a serious option to consider, especially as your business begins to grow. Licensing is fantastic as you get paid while others are working on your behalf. Licensing allows you to have partners and tap into an existing system. The more well known your brand becomes the greater the value it has. That allows you to make more money from a merchandising opportunity. Initial merchandising products may include t-shirts, hats, socks, jackets, pants and so forth.

More authors should consider endorsements deals as an additional stream of revenue. During a music conference I was introduced to a multi-platinum music producer who was promoting his new book. The producer informed me that he was endorsing one of the major music equipment company's products. As part of the agreement he was paid a set amount of money every time he spoke at a conference and mentioned the companies name. He told me that he endorsed several other companies, some of which paid for his travel arrangements from conference to conference. Endorsement deals are great because you can get behind products and services that you have been using for years. Companies are always seeking new ways to introduce and keep their products and services in front of their target market. Think of all the things you use. Your cell phone, internet access, computer products, the food you eat, clothes you were, cologne or perfume you use and so forth are but a short list of potential companies that may back your book tour or workshop series. You may be just the person to provide a solution to a companies marketing and promotions problem.

When considering obtaining a federal trademark, merchandising rights and endorsement deals you will want to seek the services of an intellectual or entertainment attorney. You may find a list of physical mailing addresses, phone and fax numbers, emails and websites to entertainment attorneys in both my books the *Atlanta Music Industry Connection and Los Angeles Music Industry Connection.* You may order these books using the order form in the back of this book or by downloading them either at **gojawar.com** or **gomusicconnection.com**.

LICENSING YOUR WORKS

The tenth source of revenue from your existing book will be through licensing your intellectual property. Licensing involves giving an individual, company or organization the rights to use your copyrighted material. A gentleman had contacted me about co-authoring a new book. After our second meeting it was decided that I would grant him a license to use some of my work found in my book the *Atlanta Music Industry Connection.* The deal was structured were he would pay a deposit for permission to use my material. I would receive a portion of the royalties from future book sells. The gentleman would be responsible for marketing and distributing the new book. Essentially, I would have greatly benefited from the deal because my work had already been completed. The gentleman would have significantly benefited because he would have had an existing product that could have assisted him with getting to market very fast. The deal was structured to be a win/win scenario for both of us. Although, the deal was never finalized I learn a number of lessons. First, know your value and worth. Second, be able to assign a monetary value to your worth. Third, it is a great idea to consult with your attorneys before signing any agreements. Fourth, be able to walk away from a deal, but leave room to reopen the discussion at some unspecified time in the future.

In addition to individuals, companies and organizations may be interested in licensing your intellectual property. This licensing arrangement may be for a number of different opportunities including foreign licensing, translation rights, republishing your works and as mentioned earlier: documentaries, direct to video, cable TV and major film & independent releases. The internet has made it feasible for a self-published author to build global contacts in an effort to expand their reach. Excellent as it is, many people are not tapping into the international markets. Through the internet you could build relationships in an effort to license your intellectual property in foreign territories.

Additionally, you will want to consider having your book translated to other languages. The Spanish speaking community is the fastest growing segment in the U.S. It would be wise to make your books available in Spanish. This will help secure your future and ensure that you have other markets which to promote your book, especially when you think your book has run its course.

WHAT YOU DIDN'T KNOW TO ASK ABOUT SELF-PUBLISHING?

WHERE WILL I SELL THE MOST BOOKS?

Although most people will ask you if your books are sold at one of the major chains like Barns & Noble, Books-A-Million or Borders the majority of your sells will most likely come directly from you. This is especially true as you do readings, speaking engagements and sit on panel discussions. You have the opportunity to sell a lot of books in the back of the room from impulsive buys. Another bulk of your sales will come from your website, given it is designed and promoted properly. Generating sells from your site is excellent, because you literally can make money while you sleep. In addition, your site allows you to have direct contact with your fans. There are a number of ways that you can sell your book from your site. First, you could take credit card orders over a secure site and ship books as orders come in. Second, you may refer buyers to another site where your book may be purchased. You may direct visitors to the amazon.com page where your book is being sold. Last, you could send visitors to another company that prints your books on demand. Meaning your books are only printed when orders are placed. Print-on-demand has become fairly popular among authors and self-publishers not wanting to get larger quantities of books printed at one time. However, print-on-demand services tend to charge a premium when printing your books. Our company offers short run printing at competitive rates. For a quote contact us at 800-963-0949.

HOW DO I GET MY BOOK INTO STORES?

"Stores" may be major chains, local bookstores and specialty retail shops. Barnes & Noble, Borders and Books-A-Million are probably the three largest chain bookstores in the United States., while amazon.com is the largest internet based bookstore in the world. Barnes & Noble, Borders, Books-A-Million and Amazon.com all give details about the process of getting your books sold in their stores. In addition, they give information that will allow your book to be sold on their websites. It is important to note that your book may be sold on one of the three major chain bookstores websites, but not necessarily in their stores. Given that you follow exactly what they suggest, you should have little problem getting your book sold through one of the major chain bookstores. It does not hurt to build a working relationship with the local bookstore manager as they sometimes have discretion as to what they will sell in the store, especially when it comes to local authors. Major chain store managers often take a special interest in local authors.

Another way to get your book sold in major chains is by going through a distributor or wholesaler. A distributor or wholesaler will either purchase the books from you or buy the books on consignment. One of the most important things you will need to do after securing distribution is to ensure that your books have been entered into the Books-In-Print Database. This will enable the publishing industry including major chain bookstores, suppliers and libraries, etc. to get details about your book. Entering your title in the Books-In-Print Database is achieved by completing the Advance Book Information (ABI) through R.R. Bowker at www.bowkerlink.com

Getting your book sold in local or independent bookstores is a fairly straightforward process. You will approach the owner or store manager and let them know that you have a new book and you are interested in placing the book in their store. You will give them a brief summary about the book. Your summary should be no more than 45 to 60 seconds. This summary should be consistent with the details on your one-sheet, flyers and the back of your book. Remember you have already done the hard work at this point- you are merely reiterating what you have written. Some local bookstores will buy the books directly from you. However most of them will choose to put the book on consignment. Most bookstores will choose to take your books on consignment because it reduces their liability. Consignment is when the store pays you after your book has sold. Consignment should not be of great concern to you, because you should have a written a masterpiece. More importantly, you should have a detailed marketing plan that will encourage readers to go to bookstores and buy your book.

HOW MANY BOOKS SHOULD I PUT IN A STORE?

Because you probably have limited money supply and resources, you will want to limit the number of books you put in each store. You will want to always have a small inventory of books on hand for those unannounced special occasions where you could quickly sell books to friends, relatives and business associates. Some stores will sell your books a lot faster by the sheer fact they have a higher degree of foot traffic in their store. Bookstores in malls for example, tend to have a lot of people going in and out of them. Especially if they are located near the food court or the main mall entrance. Until you know which stores will sell the most books in the shortest time period, you'll want to limit the number of books you put in each store. Initially, I would suggest putting between 3 to 5 books per store. This will ensure that you have enough inventory to cover many of your local book and specialty stores. As your books begin selling well in certain stores you may want to increase the amount of books you leave to anywhere from 5 to 12.

When the storeowner or manager wants to buy the books outright, of course you want them to buy as many books as they want. Always give independent bookstores something extra when they buy a certain quantity from you. That something could be an extra book, a thank you card, a gift card or t-shirt. As a service provider you always want to do more to stay in good graces... plus what goes around comes around.

Here is a little secret: by limiting the amount of books you put in every store you can create the illusion that your book is everywhere. In some cases you may even put one book in a store as I did with the first edition of the *Atlanta Music Industry Connection* Book. When you send an e-blast informing your readers or putting up a listing on your website of all the stores where your book may be bought you increase the illusion that your book is everywhere. Some people only want to buy things if they are hot or in vogue at the time. Remember readers are not aware that you may only have one book in a store at a time. All they know is that your book may be bought at X number of locations. After a few months, you should begin to see which stores sell how many books in any given time frame. As you make your assessment you should adjust your inventory levels per store as needed.

HOW DO I GET PEOPLE TO BUY MY BOOKS?

That's simple, you ask people to buy your book. I have sold a number of books by asking people to support me. However, I will admit that I'd often present the book to be of great use to others. Frequently, suggesting that the book could be given away as a gift. Whatever your book was meant to do, entertain, educate or motivate that message must be conveyed in every publicity, marketing and promotions campaign that you facilitate. People must be aware that the book exist, know its content and focus and the book must be easily accessible.

As a new author you will need to do a lot of face time. That means holding workshops, readings and book signings. You will need to have a presence and be wherever your target market frequents. That includes attending social events, conferences and having marketing materials prominently displayed. You must have no shame in your efforts of promoting a number one best seller.

HOW DO I COLLECT MONEY FROM STORES?

The best way to get your money from stores is by hiring the mob. Of course, I'm just kidding, so don't do anything silly, illegal or otherwise infringe upon the well being of your fellow citizen.

Upfront, invoice and consignment money are three ways you will get paid from stores that sell your books. Upfront money means you will receive either cash or check from the store upon delivery of your books. The day you bring in your books is the day the store pays you. I always prefer this type of money, however, most stores do not operate like this- so be pleasantly surprised when they do. When you have a store that pays you upfront make sure that you do something for the store. It could be something as small as offering to distribute some of their flyers. You may even list the store as a preferred retailer on your website, flyer and other promotional material.

Invoicing is my second choice on how to get paid from stores. Essentially, the store is paying you for your books, but they send you the money at a later date say 30, 60 or 90 days out. Invoice money is generally good as long as the store pays you when they say they're going to pay you. I have heard horror stories of how some publishers had not been paid from bookstores. Honestly, this has never been my experience. I often wonder if the publishers had an effective system in place for getting paid. Most computers come pre-installed with a Microsoft Application that allows you to easily create invoice documents.

Consignment is where you leave your books with the retailer to sell for a pre-determined price. For instance, you may sell your book to the store for $8.00 and the store may resell your book for $14.95. Once your book is actually sold to a customer, then you are due your $8.00 from the store. You are paid your money only after your product is sold. While it is always advantageous to get your money up front from retailers, most stores will choose to put your book on consignment. After your book has demonstrated a degree of success, some stores will opt to buy your books outright from you.

Getting paid from your distributor works in the same fashion as getting paid from the retailers. You will either get paid upfront, (typically by check not cash), by invoicing the distributor or by consignment. However, keep in mind that a major difference between distributors and retailers is distributors typically reserve the option of returning unsold books, (even if the goods come back damaged- damn now that's a trip.)

DO I NEED TO HAVE A WEBSITE?

Having a website is like having a mailing address. Not having a website, especially if you are a self-published author is simply not up for debate. The question is not if you should have a website, but what should your website have and how should your promote it. Your website should serve a particular function or functions. It should be directly related to your vision and mission statement.

With that being said your website should serve as the resource center for you and your books. The site should act as the ultimate promotional tool and revenue generator. It should allow users to read more about you the author and your books. In addition, your site may have details on ordering your books and becoming a part of your online community. For a list of all the websites I maintain visit **gojawar.com**. Most of the make money online sites found at **gojawar.com** will give you a list of resources and links to start your own site. The Make Money Self Publishing Kit will have a list of resources and links that allow you to create a professional website. You may download the Make Money Self Publishing Kit at **makemoneyselfpublishing.com**.

WHEN SHOULD I BEGIN PROMOTING MY BOOK?

Your marketing and promotions campaign should start long before the ink dries on the paper. You want to always brand yourself as a business entity, publicize news worthy events and market relentlessly. Because you will be promoting to different markets while setting up your distribution network, you will need to plan far in advance on when to promote your book. You'll be marketing your book to retailers, consumers and libraries attempting to get them to preorder your books. To get your books into the library system you will want to contact Quality Books- their number is 815-732-4450.

HOW LONG SHOULD I PROMOTE MY BOOK?

Your book should be promoted forever. Your books are intellectual property. It may be leased, sold, rented like real property or real estate. Your book may be licensed to others, even after you believe it has run its course. Because it is property it should be factored into your estate planning much like houses, businesses and other assets are. Your book may be passed on to your children, grandchildren or some other benefactor. The idea is that the more you promote your work the greater the market value. One easy way to ensure that you promote older titles is by mentioning them whenever you author a new book. Another way to promote previously released books is by including them on your website. Remember your site is a store that never closes and it is open to the global market. Your book should be promoted forever.

WHAT IS A ONE-SHEET?

A one-sheet is an industry standard document used to inform retailers, wholesalers, libraries and distributors about a new book release. One-sheets typically include the following: book cover artwork, ISBN and barcode numbers, suggested retail price, book distributor contact details for ordering, wholesale prices and special author mention. For example, the special author mention might read that the writer of this book is an award winning actor or filmmaker or the author has been featured on the Oprah Winfrey Show twice in one month. The "author mention" is anything that will give the book hype and build credibility.

Be mindful that you may have different one-sheets. You may have a one-sheet that is targeted specifically toward libraries. As such, you would not include the wholesale rates; rather you would include the retail list price and the distributor contact details. Likewise your retailer one-sheet may include the wholesale rate, retail list price and your contact information if you are selling directly to the bookstore. However, you may include the distributors contact information if the store is to order from your supplier.

WHAT HAPPENS TO RETURNED BOOKS?

It would be wise to read the fine print of your agreement with your distributor or wholesaler. Many times the agreement will state that 100% of books ordered may be returned to the publisher (i.e. you.) The worse part is the distributor or wholesaler may return books that are not sellable and your account instantly is in the negative. This happens if the distributor or wholesaler pays you for books ordered and returns them at a later date. This should motivate you to concentrate on smaller, frequent, non-traditional and larger non-traditional institution book sells. These non-tradtional institutions will help you maintain and grow a consistent cash flow. Remember the old saying: "never put all your eggs in one basket"- this is a sure fire reason not to.

HOW DO I PROTECT MYSELF?

1. Own and control your copyrights
2. Own and control your publishing
3. Own and control the rights, name, and likeness to your pen name and image (trademark & servicemark your stage name) Own and control your domain name. For instance, own www.yourstagename.com
4. Always have a competent literary, book publishing or entertainment attorney review and draft your contracts.
5. Attempt not to sign long-term exclusive contracts; if you do, you better do number four.
6. Create multiple streams of revenue. In this book, I have listed ten ways to make money from your book. These ten ways are also available in my audio book *Ten Ways to Make Money from Your Book.*

HOW DO I FIND INVESTORS FOR MY BOOK?

Save, beg, borrow, but don't steal. Get a second job. Replace your luxury spending like cable TV, cigarettes and alcohol, clubbing every week, eating out and shopping with putting money into your publishing company and writing career.

The truth is that most savvy investors are not going to invest their money in the book industry unless they are involved in the business of publishing books. The reason is that there are too many uncontrollable variables, which makes investing in the publishing industry a bit risky compared to other investment opportunities. However, someone who knows the business may be more willing to invest in your venture. Keep in mind, however, that you probably will not maintain control of your ideal or intellectual property unless the investor views you as an equal. Meaning that although *they* may put up the money, *you* may have built a strong brand in the marketplace. Seemingly if you have the ability to walk away from the deal, it puts you in a great position because you have options (or at least the *perception* that you have options.)

Most importantly, you should build your brand, whereas you become extremely marketable. Everyone wants to be a part of the winning team. Everyone wants to be around success. If you prove in the marketplace that you have started that winning team or successful business system, investors will seek you out, because you have a proven track record.

To get money from an investor you must first begin to think as an investor. As an investor you would ask yourself at least some of the following questions:

1. Would I rather invest in an individual or a business system?
2. Would I invest in someone who has not invested in themselves?
3. Would I invest my money in something tangible like real estate or an author?
4. What are the risks associated with investing with this person or business?
5. What is the profit potential for investing with this person or business?
6. What is the most secure way to invest my money while seeking the highest return?
7. What is the rate of return on my investment?
8. Does this person or business have a track record in what they are attempting to do?
9. Is this person or business respected in their industry?
10. How much control will I have in the business after I right the check?

Before seeking investors you will want to have a track record and have invested some of your monies to show that you are serious about your book and publishing company. While not advisable, I know of authors who have used personal credit cards to get their seed money. Some of the ways of getting your seed money may include getting a second job or replacing your luxury spending like cable TV, buying cigarettes and alcohol, clubbing every week, eating out and shopping with putting money into your publishing career.

WHAT IS RECOUPMENT?

The term "recoupment" is not really applicable to a self-published author. However, at some point you may consider getting a publishing deal through another publishing house. "Recoupment" is when a publisher or investor has to get back their initial investment from an author's book. This initial investment is called "an advance." Authors will not receive any royalties until the publisher has recouped their initial investment. As a self-published author you are the investor and will need to recoup your initial investment. Many authors are excited about the advance that they receive from a publisher, but what happens if you don't recoup? If you don't recoup the publisher may release you from you agreement. However, they'll normally retain the rights to your manuscript. By the publisher retaining your rights, you are unable to license the book to someone else. Depending on how restricted your agreement is- you may not be able to take, say a novel and turn it into a movie, DVD or e-book. Be mindful of recoupment when signing a publishing contract. You will need to consult with a literary or entertainment attorney before signing any agreement.

What You Need To Know About Self-Publishing?

CREATING A SYSTEM

Everything you do from how you write your book, to cover designed, layout and pricing, channels of distribution and promotions will need to have an effective and efficient system. You will want to take existing systems and mold them to fit your needs. Creating an effective system is extremely important. A system will allow you to tackle obstacles before they happen, improve customer service, production, manage growth and increase your money pipeline or cash flow.

Systems are so important that our very existence depends on them. Think about all the wonderful systems around us... the system of moving from night to day, the system of the human body, the system of an automobile, the system of reproduction, the system of growing and harvesting food, the system of transporting people and goods, the system of human growth and development, the system for raising a child and the system for building a community and nation.

When I published my first book, I found myself selling out of the book faster than I had anticipated. Initially, I thought this was a great thing. After all, if I'm selling out of books, I'm moving inventory and making money (or atleast that is what I thought.) By me running out of inventory I was unable to quickly stock stores with more books, which meant readers were unable to get the product they wanted when they wanted it. This meant that customers were unhappy, stores where unhappy and I was unhappy, what a lousy way to do business. I had to implement a system that allowed me to deal with this opportunity. I had an opportunity to make readers happy, stores happy and myself happy- what a wonderful situation! After creating and implementing a system, readers and stores where rarely without books. Being an author and publisher you will truly have to have a system to ensure your success. My company provides printing, book publishing, consulting and coaching services with an emphasis on strategic planning, branding and execution. To get started call 1-800-963-0949.

COVER, BACK & SPINE DESIGN

I will not attempt to explain the technical points of designing your book cover; we will leave that to the graphic artist. I will give you exercises for you develop of your book cover concept, which you may relay to your graphic artist. Your book cover should accomplish a few goals. First, it should quickly grab your target markets attention. The book cover should immediately grab the eye, like the boogieman grabs a child. The colors, pictures and lettering style and size all determine the overall look and feel of your book.

How do you design a catchy book cover? Take a few of the books in your personal library and place them on a table. Carefully examine the covers that immediately grab your attention. Ask yourself why do these books grab your eye over others? Is it the coloring, the style of font, the size of font, the pictures, the title, sub-title or all of the above? Now turn these books over and repeat the exercise with the back of the books. Which ones immediately grab your attention, which ones are easiest to read, which ones hold your attention the longest? Is it the coloring, the style or size of font? Does it make a bit of difference if the author's picture is on the back cover or not as to which book grabs and holds your attention most? Now place these books on your bookshelf with the spine facing out. Which of the book spines immediately gets your attention? Why do these particular book spines catch your eye? Is it the coloring, the style of font, the size of font, the pictures, the title, sub-title or all of the above?

You will want to repeat this process of examining books. This time you will want to go to a few different libraries and bookstores and look at books in the same genre you plan to publish. What book spines cause you to pick the book off the shelf? What book cover draws you to open the book, thumb through the pages and look at the back cover? This is the same process book buyers go through when seeking a novel, fiction, children's, technical or how to book, but don't have any particular title in mind.

Visit amazon.com, bn.com and borders.com and conduct a search for books in the genre you are writing. Look at the covers on these websites and ask yourself which books immediately catch your eye? Examine the covers using the same method explained above. These exercises of looking at book covers both offline and on should give you ideas for designing your own cover.

Your cover design may mirror the title or theme of your book. If your book were on finance or investing you may have images of dollars, yen or some other currency. If your book was a guide on investing in the stock market you may want to include ticker symbols on the front cover. In many instances less is more. Big, bold, catchy titles normally always win, given your title is direct and specific.

A book's barcode should be placed at the bottom right hand corner on the back of the book. The books category(s) should be placed in the top left hand corner on the back of the book. My music industry books category reads "Music/Business/Directory". Placing the subject(s) on the type left hand corner makes it easy for stores and libraries to put your book in the correct section on the shelf.

Second, the texture of paper and whether the book is a soft or hardcover will add or take away from the book. It will immediately describe the type of book you have written. All textbooks I have seen in hardcover, whereas, novels and fantasy books tend to be paperback. Children books come in both hard and paperback formats. Of course, if a children's book is meant for the child to read, it normally is hardback with vibrant lettering and colors. Third, the title of your book should do one of the following things: It should easily describe the contents of your book, answer a question, draw curiosity, mystery or controversy. If your book is a resource tool, directory or how to guide for music professionals engaged in the Atlanta Music Scene, it may read the *Atlanta Music Industry Connection: Resources for Artists, Producers and Managers.* If your book discusses how to make money in the business of music, it may read *How to Get Paid in the Record Game by Raheem.*

What do you think a book titled *Murder by Injection* would be about? More importantly, does the title alone evoke curiosity and mystery? I think it does. The title caught my attention and caused me to read it. The title sounds like a mystery novel. However, the subtitle *the Story of Medical Conspiracy Against America* set the overall tone for the book. The entire book title may now be considered controversial and draw curiosity instead of being a mystery novel. *Super Power!* Now that is a title that will evoke controversy and curiosity. However, beware that your title may make it difficult for your book to be sold in chain bookstores like Barnes & Noble, Borders, and Books-A-Million. To get your book covers designed, call Ashil at 404-351-4312. Tell Ashil you found him in *How to Self-Publish for Profit* Book by JaWar.

GRAPHIC DESIGN COMPANIES

- Blaze 1 Graphixs
  4548 Howell Farms Rd., Ackworth, GA 30303
  P) 770-975-0522
  www.blaze1graphixs.com

- Creative Juice
  6303 Chastain Drive NE, Atlanta, GA 30342
  P) 404-851-1685 F) 404-851-1684
  dvsjuice@aol.com

- Design Apart
  P) 404-351-4312
  Design Apart has designed several of my book covers.

- Eboni Graphix
  3350 Riverwood Parkway, Suite 1900
  Atlanta, GA 30339
  P) 678-354-9078 F) 678-354-3997
  www.eboni-graphix.com
  lbeverly@eboni-graphix.com

- ➤ Green Designs
  5744 Norman Ct., College Park, GA 30349
  P) 404-388-6888 F) 770-991-0120
  www.greendesigns.org
  tgreen@greendesigns.org

- ➤ I Design Graphics
  4600 Cascade Rd., Atlanta, GA 30331
  P) 404-505-1443 F) 404-691-5209
  www.ithanpaynecreative.com
  ithanpayne@aol.com

- ➤ Jamire
  P.O. Box 492494, College Park, GA 30349
  P) 866-629-3475 P) 404-403-2729
  www.jamire.com
  tcarpenter@jamire.com

- ➤ Moz Graphics
  4120 Jeffrey Dr., College Park, GA 30349
  P) 404-849-3220
  www.mozgraphics.com

- ➤ New World Group
  1117 Peachtree Walk, Suite 123, Atlanta, GA 30309
  P) 404-876-6366
  www.nwgsite.com

- ➤ One 3 Creative
  565 Dutch Valley Rd., Atlanta, GA 30324
  P) 404-872-30324

- ➤ Sigmoe Media Group
  1715 Jasmine Circle Unite 18103, Atlanta, GA 30315
  P) 404-849-1157
  www.sigmoemediagroup.com
  cedric@sigmoemediagroup.com

BOOK LAYOUT

A well-designed book layout will ensure that someone looking at your book for the first time can quickly locate what he or she is looking for. Have you ever been in the bookstore or library and picked up a title because of how it looked? We all have. The book that had a good layout probably kept you reading, because it was easy to find what you were looking for. More importantly, it was "easy on your eyes" and did not make them tired. A poorly designed book layout will ensure that first time readers put your book down just as fast as they picked it up. There is a book on self-publishing that caught my attention, but I couldn't read it long enough to see if I wanted to buy it. You see the fonts throughout the book were varying in size. There didn't appear to be any consistency as it related to the font size and style; and while there may have been, I couldn't figure it out. I ended up buying two different books on self-publishing. Although, I wanted the other book (partially because it was priced right) I didn't purchase it.

In addition, to capturing the attention of first time readers, a well-designed book layout will ensure that your readers are comfortable re-reading your book. This is important because you want people to read your book over and over. The more people read something the more they internalize or become entertained by it. As this happens, they will undoubtedly tell others about your book and word of mouth promotion is the best form of promotion you could ask for.

BOOK PRICING

We are all price sensitive to products and services that we buy. Book buyers are no different. Especially, if there are similar books on the market. There are a few things you will want to consider when pricing your book. First, you must make a profit. That means consider your production, printing and marketing cost. In addition, factor in your time and energy in writing and researching your book. Second, your book should be competitively price. Visit your local bookstore and amazon.com and see what other books in your genre are selling for. Your book should cost around the same price. The retail price of your book should end in 95 or 99 cents. For instance, the price may be $19.95 or $14.95. Studies have shown that $19.95 and $14.95 look a lot smaller than 20 or 15 respectively. You will also want to price your book near increments of 5. This will make it easier to deal in cash when you sell books at your speaking engagements, festivals, conferences, parties and conventions. For instance, price your book at $4.95, $9.95, $14.95, $19.95, $24.95 and so on. Third, the pricing of your book should have bookstores and distributors in mind. Bookstores typically want a 40% markup from the wholesale price. Another way of looking at it is the bookstores typically want a 40% discount off the list price. So, if the cover or retail price of your book were $19.95 the store would expect to buy the book at $11.97 or receive a discount of $7.98 off the cover price. Distributors seek and even greater discount than do bookstores. The reason is that they are the ones selling to the stores; therefore they must be able to sell the book to the stores at a price that the store will expect to receive.

Distributors seek anywhere from a 50% or greater discount on books.

You might be thinking this takes a lot of your profit margin- and it does. However, if you are a self-published author, the majority of your sales will not come from chain bookstores. Rather, they will come from your speaking engagements, special events and your website.

CHANNELS OF DISTRIBUTION

As a self-publisher you are in a unique position to create multiple streams of revenue from one book. This is directly related to your channels of distribution. Your book should be sold through the following outlets: your website, bookstores, specialty stores, independent distributors, festivals, at conferences, concerts, out the trunk, your backpack, book clubs and so forth.

I would seek distribution in major chains like Barnes & Noble Borders and Books-A-Million mainly for the sake of just having books placed there. By making your books available in major chain stores, you add credibility to your publishing house. I have found that for many people it is a legitimizing factor. Some people don't think your book is "a book" unless it is sold in a major chain store- even if the book is in their very hands and they are reading it. Distribution is also great for having your books sold through colleges, universities and public libraries.

You will want to deal directly with local bookstores and specialty shops in your area. The reason is two fold. First, you have the opportunity to mold a system that will work best for you and your publishing house. Second, neighborhood bookstore owners are typically very receptive to local authors and want to see them do well. After all, it would give them great bragging rights to say that they helped you get started before being featured on Oprah or having a best seller.

Two of the largest book wholesalers/distributors in the United States are Ingram and Baker & Taylor. Ingram may be contacted at 800-937-8000; Baker & Taylor may be called at 800-775-1100.

RETAIL READY

To create a "retail ready" book means your book should conform to or at least have the minimum standard currently used by the book publishing industry. Today that includes copyrighting your book through the U.S. Library of Congress, having your book perfectly bound, having an ISBN Number, a price and a barcode on the back bottom right hand corner of your book. In addition, you'll want the Library of Congress Control Number, copyright date, first date of publication, country of printing, author and publisher details on the copyright page. The Library of Congress Control Number makes it easier to have your books sold in public library systems. However, it is not mandatory to have a Control Number in order to conform to minimum book publishing industry standards.

YOU CAN'T BE AN INTROVERT

I've met authors whose books have been in print for over twelve months. When I ask the author how their book is doing, they tell me it is doing "ok", but it is only in two stores. Are you serious? That *can't* be so... Those people are scared to get out there and market and sell their books. Books, like other goods, generally have to be pushed before they will sell at the retail level. As a self-published author you are the best form of promotions you have. You have to tell everyone you know and, more importantly, those you don't about your book. As a reminder: I am the author of the *Atlanta Music Industry Connection* Book. It is a great resource tool and has the most comprehensive contact list of Atlanta Music Business Professionals in print. As people we tend to feed off the excitement of others. As an introvert- you will need to change your personality if your book is to see any success. Readers, retailers, distributors and anyone dealing with you will quickly determine if your book is worth reading based on your enthusiasm. Once, your book starts selling you'll really need to drum up your excitement.

Surround yourself with high-energy persons and learn how they interact with others. Study them and then become an active player in high-level communications. Plan on meeting five new people a day. Meeting may simply mean introducing yourself and letting those people know that you are a published author by giving them your flyer or business card promoting your book. Given that you meet five new people a day, you would have introduced yourself to 150 people in a month's time. At the end of twelve months you would have introduced yourself to roughly one thousand eight hundred twenty five (1,825) people. By doing this, you automatically brand yourself and promote your book on an ongoing basis. You will force yourself to become an active player in high-level communications, thereby increasing your windows of opportunity.

YOU MUST BECOME AN EXPERT

If your book is a "how to" book, you must become an expert in your field. Believe it or not, you will become an expert in the eyes of many of your readers. Be sure that your information is accurate and complete, as people will hold you to what is in print. By writing a how to resource you may be asked to appear on radio or tv and interviewed in print media. This is a great way to solidify your position in your market and prove why readers should get a copy of your book. You will want to attend conferences and events where your target market will frequent. I would frequent model calls, independent film festivals and fashion shows. Most people did not see the value in my attending these events, but I understood that these varying industries are all entertainment based. More importantly, many of the people in film, fashion and modeling either want to be in the music biz, are in the music biz or know someone in the music biz. Increasing my sales at these events helps solidify me being a key player in the music business and book publishing worlds.

YOUR FIRST BOOK MAY MAKE YOU RICH

More than likely your first book will not make you financially rich- but it may make you rich in other areas of life. My first book the *Atlanta Music Industry Connection* allowed me free entry into many nightclubs, exclusive industry parties, networking activities and positioned me above other music consultants in the business. It afforded me opportunities to speak at high schools, colleges and universities, music conferences and public libraries. Because of my first book, I was able to position myself to leave a low paying job that was draining my spirit. You see I am a writer, artist and now author and needed to be free like a bird in the sky. Most importantly, I was able to help change the lives of others by providing contacts, practical information and inspiration to those with little to no direction in life or their music careers. It is this same spirit that has guided me to write this book on book publishing for those who desire to see their writing in print.

Your book should open doors for you. Through proper planning your first book will afford you opportunities to write and publish more books. It will also create multiple streams of revenue through speaking engagements, endorsement deals, licensing and merchandising rights. What good is the money you will generate if you are not healthy and happy and willing to create a plan of plans to give it all back in this lifetime?

IT AIN'T THAT HARD

Some people think that self-publishing is more difficult than getting a publishing deal. The truth of the matter is that both opportunities require the writer to market their book. The difference is that the self-published author maintains the rights to their copyrights and is in position to earn much more money over the long haul. Self-publishing is made easy by following the steps below.

First, create a plan of action. Your plan should include things that you are able to do with little to know help from others. The plan should consider adding more people to your team as your business system grows. Second, you must have a practical marketing and promotions plan. The marketing plan will need to include promotions on a recurring basis. Your efforts should bring awareness to your book and drive sells. At the end of the day your marketing, promotions and publicity efforts should drive people to buy your book. People rarely buy new products they are unfamiliar with. For most authors the difficult part is in marketing themselves and their books. If you are to be a successful author you will have to promote yourself. As you do this, people will buy your books. Given that your books are a great read and are readily available, word of mouth promotions will encourage others to buy. While self-publishing is not hard, it does require vision, burning desire, a written plan and daily execution.

Since you are reading this, you have already taken steps to becoming a victorious writer, author and publisher. Stay on your grind, continue to hustle and build your business. I have created a number of audio books so you may listen to some of this information while on the go. The audio book titles include What You Didn't Know to Ask about Self-Publishing, Ten Ways to Make Money from Your Book, What You Need to Know about Self-Publishing and Getting Book Distribution. For ordering details complete the order form in the back of this book.

NO ONE CARES ABOUT YOUR BOOK BUT YOU

Despite that it may have taken years to write your first book or that you feel the information will dramatically improve someone else's life, no one really cares about your book but you! Unless you tell them- people won't know what you have been through or what really motivated you to write your book. The readers may be concerned about how your book may entertain them allowing them to escape their realities or how your book may help them solve one or more of their problems. By focusing your marketing efforts on how your book will entertain or help someone solve a problem, you greatly increase the chances that readers will take interest in your writing. As people become familiar with you and your books they will began to be fans. As this happens, they will promote you for free by telling others about your work. On the other hand, by maintaining the idea that no one cares about your book, but you, will help you preserve the eye of the tiger and relentless winning spirit in your promotions campaign.

YOUR STORY WAS MEANT TO BE SOLD

Your story was meant to be sold. You were given a thought or vision. Someone or something inspired you. You took the time to write your thoughts in either a very creative story format or how to guide. You completed the necessary research to create your book. You may have even gotten your books printed, but what good does it do if know one knows they're available. Books were meant to be read. Your book was meant to be sold.

STOP WASTING TIME; GET STARTED

One of my friends had been working on a book for a few years, he conducted a great deal of research. His book contained interviews and contacts. The book had all the right stuff. He promoted it through word-of-mouth advertising, distributing flyers, email blast and on his website. The hype machine had been created and was working. People were talking about his book. While I did not see the manuscript I was confident that the book would be a great read. I, like everyone else, was ready to buy my copy in support and to learn from this well respected figure. My friend and I would talk from time to time and he would share additions and deletions of his book with me. Every idea he had seemed to be a great one. I would always think to myself: "Wow! His book is really going to be received well by readers."

Although I started working on my book the *Atlanta Music Industry Connection* after my friends, my book hit the bookstores before his did. He would often give me words of encouragement, ways to improve the next edition of my book and how I might enhance the book through creative synergies with other companies.

At some point you must get started. First, you'll need to consider why you are writing, who will be your audience and how will you reach that audience. Second, you'll need to begin brainstorming, writing as it comes, slowly putting together your thoughts like you would a jig saw puzzle. While you are writing you will want to simultaneously write out your marketing and promotions plans. You will want to refer to my audio book *Ten Steps to Successful Book Promotions.*

My friend is not the only author and publisher who takes an abundance of time to release his/her book. Many of you have been considering writing and publishing your work, but have not done so. Remember your story is too important to continue collecting dust in the basement, attic or garage. Your story is too important to wait for another publishing house's approval. Your story is too important to wait for the approval of an agent. Your story is too important for you to let fear stop you from achieving your goals and realizing your success.

It is time to do as you were meant to do; take control of your own destiny and fulfill your dreams of becoming a successful published author. Your book may save a life, inspire another and bring you unparalleled happiness, but only if you take action today! You should get started immediately as you have already wasted too much time. My company offers printing, book publishing, consulting and coaching services with an emphasis on strategic planning, branding and implementation. To get started give us a call at 1-800-963-0949.

SELLING CEASES WHEN YOU STOP EATING

I enjoy selling my books. After all, my books are a snap picture of my thoughts, research and contacts at a particular moment in time. For me selling ensures that more people constantly read my thoughts. More importantly it increases the chances that I can impact someone else's life in a major way. Selling my book only stops when I'm ready to stop eating. I attempt to always have flyers and a few books on me at all times, especially during the spring and summer seasons. Sometimes I pop up on an outdoor festival or park event where there are a lot of people. This is a great opportunity to promote and sell my print and audio books. As the saying goes: "if you stay ready you don't have to get ready."

As a self-published author you have to be relentless about moving your product, being able to turn a casual conversation into a sale. Every time you do- your skills will improve. We all tend to do business with people that we are familiar with. Book buyers are no different. As you go about your day, talk with strangers, many of them will support you in your efforts by buying a book, even if they are not interested in what you do. Attempt not to make quick assumptions about strangers. I have often asked older women if they would be interested in supporting me by buying one of my books under the Music Industry Connection Book Series. While some of them have said no, many of them have said yes. Some of them have bought the book as a gift for someone, for themselves or simply because they respected what I was doing. It is much easier to sell to people who you easily identify with, but it is when you are able to sell to a different demographic that ensures you continued success and growth. Remember selling ceases only when you stop eating.

Through my other self-publishing audio and print book series you will learn how to create greater opportunities for yourself. I have created a system and step-by-step process that will help you sell more books. You may contact me at 1-800-963-0949 to set-up a one-on-one consultation or to book me for a speaking engagement. Visit **gojawar.com** to view videos I created about self-publishing and making money online.

PROMOTIONS IS FOREVER

Promotions are an ongoing process. One way of ensuring that you always have promotional tools is to get a minimum number of flyers or business cards printed either every month or every other month. I get 5,000 full color flyers printed per month. This guarantees I continue to brand and market my books month after month and quarter after quarter. It also forces me to think of new ways to distribute my flyers and expand my reach, as I don't want to have too many flyers at my disposal. Our company provides flyer printing; give us a call at 800-963-0949 for a quote.

Having a well designed website allows you to promote your book to the world 24/7. A well designed website will include a few of the key elements. First, your site should load fast-meaning it should be easy for people to get to it whether they have a high-speed connection, dial up or are using a wireless PDA. Flash helps to enhance the site, but should not be overused when designing a website. Second, the pages on your site should be consistent. The color scheme, font size and style should be fairly consistent from page to page. Third, visitors should be able to navigate through a website with ease. Adding a pull down menu or search engine on every page will help you achieve this goal. Fourth, your website should be content driven. Details about your book, you, scheduled book signings and where your book may be bought will help enhance your site. Having a well designed website allows you to promote your book to the world 24/7.

As time progresses you may start to loose drive for promoting your book- particularly when you start writing your next masterpiece. Keep in mind that promotions are forever. Especially, when you have more than one book on the market. By having more than one book, you increase the chances to sell additional products to readers. There are two ways to ensure you don't loose drive in promoting your book. First, you should have a well thought out marketing plan. One of the key elements in a marketing plan is a timeline. This will ensure that even when you loose drive you are able to promote your books. Second, you'll want to promote previous releases in your new books. That seems simple enough, but most authors don't do it. Remember promotions are forever.

YOU'RE NOT JUST AN AUTHOR

Consider yourself a businessperson who writes and publishes and you will go further faster. Sorry to say, some authors believe that because they have written a book, others should buy and read it. The reality is that no one cares as much about your book as you do, especially if you are signed to a major publishing house. As someone in business, you will need to consider planning, marketing, distribution, customer service, cash flow and taxes. Because this information is not always clear to creative people, I have included ten must know and do things for any businessperson who authors books:

- Copyright your books through the Library of Congress using form TX
- Obtain a business license
- Form a business entity
- Get a Tax I.D.
- Open a business checking account
- Obtain a written business plan
- Complete a marketing plan
- Have a phone number for professional use
- Get a literary or entertainment attorney
- Get a C.P.A. or professional tax consultant

BOOK PRINTERS

I have shared with you details about copyrights, trademarks, business entities, ISBN Numbers, barcodes, cover layout design, marketing, promotions and distribution channels for your book. Given you have read and reread the information in this and other books on publishing and done research online about self-publishing, you should be just about ready to get your book printed.

To minimize your printing cost, you will want to get your first book printed in one of the following standard sizes, 5.25 X 8.25, 5.5 X 8.5, 6 X 9 or 8.5 X 11. Theses sizes are in inches. The standard paperweight for the pages inside the book is either 50lb or 60lb. While binding may be done in a number of ways, perfect bound will be your preferred choice to ensure your book looks like most the books you see sold in the bookstore. Your front and back cover may be 10 pt C1S with a matte, lamination or UV coating. A matte coating tends to have a dull look and feel, while a laminated or UV cover adds a shining look to the book and protects the book cover.

I would encourage you to visit as many book printers' websites as possible and ask for samples whenever you can. Through this process, you will learn a great deal about the various printing opportunities available to you. You can get as few as 100 books printed or as many as your pockets can afford. When contacting the companies below let them know you found them in JaWar's *How to Self-Publish for Profit Book*.

- A&A Printing, Inc.
  6103 Johns Road, Tampa, Florida 33634
  P) 813-886-0065 P) 866-886-0065 F) 813-884-0304
  www.printshopcentral.com
  info@printshopcentral.com

- Action Printing Inc.
  N6637 Rolling Meadows Drive, Fond du Lac, WI 54937
  P) 920-907-7809 F) 920-907-7996
  www.actionprinting.com

- Adibooks.com
  181 Industrial Ave., Lowell, MA 01852
  P) 978-458-2345 F) 978-458-3026
  www.adibooks.com

- ADR BookPrint
  2012 E. Northern Avenue, Wichita, KS 67216
  P) 800-767-6066 F) 316-522-5445
  adr@adrbookprint.com
  www.adrbookprint.com

- ADR BookPrint Express
  500 Century Plaza Dr, Houston, TX 77073
  P) 866-821-1200 P) 281-821-1240 F) 281-821-6386
  www.bookprintexpress.com

- All-American Printing Services
  1130 Industrial Ave, Suite 12, Petaluma, CA 94952
  P) 707-762 2500 F) 707 762 2505
  www.allamericanprinting.com

- Ames On-Demand
  30 Dane Street, Somerville, MA 02143
  P) 617-776-3360 F) 617-623-6306
  www.amesondemand.com

- ➤ Bang Printing
  1473 Highway 18 E, P.O. Box 587, Brainerd, MN 56401
  P) 218-829-2877 P) 800-328-0450 F) 218-829-7145
  bangprinting.com
  banginfo@bangprinting.com

- ➤ Berryville Graphics
  25 Jack Enders Blvd., Berryville, VA 22611
  P) 540-955-9251 P) 800-382-7249 F) 540-955-9285
  www.bvgraphics.com

- ➤ Bethany Press
  6820 W. 115th St., Bloomington, MN 55438
  P) 952-914-7400 F) 952-914-7410
  www.bethanypress.com
  info@bethanypress.com

- ➤ Book-Mart Press, Inc.
  2001 Forty Second Street, North Bergen, NJ 07047
  P) 201-864-1887 F) 201-864-7559
  www.courier.com

- ➤ BookMasters, Inc.
  2541 Ashland Road, P.O. Box 2139, Mansfield, OH 44905
  P) 800-537-6727 P) 419-589-5100 F) 419-589-4040
  www.bookmasters.com
  info@bookmasters.com

- ➤ BooksOnDemand.com
  540 Business Park Circle, Stoughton, WI 53589
  P) 608-205-9555 F) 608-873-4558
  www.booksondemand.com
  info@booksondemand.com

- ➤ BookMobile.com
  2402 University Ave West, Ste 206, St. Paul, MN 55114
  P) 651-642-9241 P) 800-752-3303 F) 651-603-9263
  www.bookmobile.com

- Boyd Printing Company, Inc.
  49 Sheridan Avenue Albany, New York 12210
  P) 800-877-2693 F) 518-436-7433
  www.boydprinting.com
  info@boydprinting.com

- Braceland
  7625 Suffolk Ave., Philadelphia, PA 19153
  P) 215-492-0200 P) 800-338-1280 F) 215-492-1348
  www.braceland.com
  info@braceland.com

- Brenner Printing
  1234 Triplett, San Antonio, TX 78216
  P) 210-349-4024 F) 210-349-1501
  brennerprinting.com
  brenner@brennerprinting.com

- C&M Press
  4825 Nome Street, Denver, CO 80239
  P) 303-375-9922 F) 303-375-8699
  www.cmpress.com

- Central Plains Book Manufacturing
  4th & C Sts. Strother Field Ind. Park
  P.O. Box 738, Arkansas City, KS 67005
  P) 877-278-2726 F) 316-221-4762
  www.centralplainsbook.com

- CJK
  3962 Virginia Ave., Cincinnati, OH 45227
  P) 800-598-7808 P) 513-7-271-6035 F) 513-271-6082
  www.cjkusa.com

- ColorCentric Corporation
  10 Carlson Road, Rochester, NY 14610
  P) 585-288-1240 F) 585-288-1671
  www.colorcentriccorp.com
  info@colorcentriccorp.com

- Color House Graphics
  3505 Eastern Ave., Grand Rapids, MI 49508
  P) 616-241-1916 F) 616-245-5494
  www.colorhousegraphics.com

- Copy-Rite Press, Inc.
  614 S. Date Avenue, Alhambra, CA 91803
  P) 626-576-1504 F) 626-289-9571
  www.copyritepress.com

- Copy Concepts, Inc.
  8080 Tristar Drive, Suite 112, Irving, TX 75063
  P) 800-644-2111 P) 214-492-2000 F) 214-492-2010
  www.copcon.com
  info@copcon.com

- Corley Printing
  3777 Rider Trail South, St. Louis, MO 63045
  P) 314-739-3777 F) 314-739-1436
  books@corleyprinting.com
  www.corleyprinting.com

- Country Press, Inc.
  1 Commercial Dr, Lakeville, MA 02347
  P) 508-947-4485 F) 508-947-8989
  www.countrypressinc.com
  customerservice@countrypressinc.com

- Courier Corp.
  5 Wellman Ave., N. Chelmsford, MA 01863
  P) 978-251-6000 F) 978-251-8228
  www.courier.com

➤ Covington Group
4050 Pennsylvania, Suite 230, Kansas City, MO 64111
P) 816-753-1988 F) 816-561-9324
www.covingtongroup.net

➤ Crane Duplicating
9 Marthas Ln, Harwich, MA 02645
P) 508-760-1601 F) 508-760-1544
www.craneduplicating.com
info@craneduplicating.com

➤ CSS Publishing
P.O. Box 4503, Lima, OH 45802-4503
http://bodbooks.com
P) 800-241-4056 P) 419-227-1818 F) 419-222-4647

➤ Cushing Malloy, Inc.
P.O. Box 8632, 1350 N. Main Street, Ann Arbor, MI 48107
P) 888-295-7244 P) 734-663-8554 F) 734-663-5731
www.cushing-malloy.com

➤ Dallas Offset
2110 Panoramic Circle, P.O. Box 223664, Dallas, TX 75212
P) 214-630-8741 F) 214-638-7796
www.dallasoffset.com

➤ Darby Printing Company
6215 Purdure Drive, Atlanta, GA 30336
P) 800-241-5292 F) 404-346-3332
www.darbyprinting.com
sales@darbyprinting.com

➤ Data Reproductions Corporation
4545 Glenmeade Lane, Auburn Hills, MI 48326
P) 248-371-3700 P) 800-242-3114 F) 248-371-3710
www.datarepro.com
kcolton@datarepro.com

- D. B. Hess & Co.
  1530 McConnel Rd., Woodstock, IL 60098
  P) 815-338-6900 F) 815-336-9608
  www.dbhess.com

- DeHart's Printing Services
  3265 Scott Blvd., Santa Clara, CA 95054
  P) 888-982-4763 P) 408-982-9118 F) 408-982-9912
  www.deharts.com
  solutions@deharts.com

- Delta Printing Solutions
  28210 N. Avenue Stanford, Valencia, CA 91355
  P) 800-32-DELTA F) 661-295-4358
  www.deltaprintingsolutions.com
  sales@deltaprintingsolutions.com

- DigiNet Printing
  5723 NW 159th St., Miami Lakes, FL 33014
  P) 305-825-9260 F) 305-825-9294
  www.diginetprinting.com

- Dome Printing
  340 Commerce Circle, Sacramento, CA 95814
  P) 916-923-3663 P) 800-343-3139 F) 916-923-9310
  www.domeprinting.com
  csr@domeprinting.com

- EBSCO Media, Publications Department
  801 - 5th Avenue South, Birmingham, AL 35233
  P) 800-765-0852 F) 205-323-1508
  www.ebscomedia.com

- Eco Printing, Inc.
  2515 Lantrac Court, Decatur, GA 30035-4006
  P) 770-322-8998
  www.ecoprinting.com

- Edwards Brothers
  2500 S. State St., Ann Arbor, MI
  P) 734-769-4756
  www.edwardsbrothers.com

- Eerdmans Printing Company
  231 Jefferson SE, Grand Rapids, MI 49503
  P) 616-451-0763 F) 616-459-4356
  www.eerdmansprinting.com

- Fidlar Doubleday
  4570 Commercial Avenue, Suite A, Portage, MI 49002
  P) 800-248-0888 F) 800-884-2437
  www.fidlardoubleday.com
  info@fidlar-doubleday.com

- G&H Soho
  117 Grand St., Hoboken, NJ 07030
  P) 201-216-9400 F) 201-216-1778
  www.ghsoho.com
  sales@ghsoho.com

- GB Printing Enterprises, Inc.
  510 Heron Drive, Suite 204, Logan Township, NJ 08085
  P) 856-241-2790 P) 877-222-1360 F) 856-241-2795
  www.gbprint.com
  sales@gbprint.com

- Giant Horse Printing, Inc.
  1336 San Mateo Avenue, South San Francisco, CA 94080
  P) 650-875-7137 F) 650-875-7194
  www.gianthorse.com
  info@gianthorse.com

- ➢ Gray Printing Company
  401 E. North Street, Fostoria, Ohio 44830
  P) 419-435-6638 P) 800-837-GRAY F) 419-435-9410
  www.grayprinting.com
  info@grayprinting.com

- ➢ Green Button Inc.
  133 Oxford St., Hanover Township, PA 18706
  P) 570-704-0334 F) 570-704-0298
  www.greenbuttoninc.com
  greenbutton@allvantage.com

- ➢ Greyden Press
  2020 Builder's Place, Columbus, OH 43204
  P) 614-488-2525 F) 614-488-2817
  www.greydenpress.com
  info@greydenpress.com

- ➢ Greene Publications, Inc.
  23 Alabama Avenue, Island Park, NY 11558
  P) 516-897-4404 F) 516-897-7767
  www.greenepublicationsinc.com

- ➢ Godar & Hossenlopp Printing Company
  151 Mitchell Ave , South San Francisco, CA 94080
  P) 415-970-0155

- ➢ Gorham Printing
  334 Harris Rd., Rochester, WA 98579
  P) 800-837-0970 F) 360-273-8679
  www.gorhamprinting.com
  info@gorhamprinting.com

- ➢ Great Impressions Printing & Graphics
  444 W. Mockingbird Lane, Dallas, TX 75247
  P) 214-631-2665 F) 214-631-4329

➤ Hagerstown Bookbinding and Printing
952 Frederick Street, Hagerstown, MD 21740
P) 800-638-3508 P) 301-733-2000 F) 301-733-6586
www.hbp.com
info@hbp.com

➤ Hart Graphics
10228 Technology Drive, Knoxville, TN 37932
P) 865-675-1600 F) 865-675-1601
www.hartgraphics.com

➤ HCI Printing & Publishing
3201 SW 15th Street, Deerfield Beach, FL 33442-8190
P) 800-851-9100 P) 954-360-0909 F) 800-424-7652
www.hcibooks.com

➤ Houston Datum
8885 Monroe, Houston, TX 77061
P) 713-944-4600 F) 713-944-0915
www.houstondatum.com

➤ Huron Valley Printing & Imaging
4557 Washtenaw Avenue, Ann Arbor, MI 48108-1011
P) 734-971-1700 F) 734-971-6420
www.hvpi.com

➤ Impressions Unlimited
2300 Windsor Court, Unit C, Addison, IL 60101
P) 630-705-6464 F) 630-7-5-1598
www.impressionsunltd.com
info@impressionsunltd.com

➤ Inland Press / Inland Book
W141 N9450 Fountain Blvd., Menoomonee Falls, WI 53051
P) 800-552-2235 P) 262-255-5800 F) 262-255-9730
www.inlandbook.com

- Integrated Book Technology, Inc.
  18 Industrial Park Road, Troy, NY 12180
  P) 518-271-5117 F) 518-266-9422
  http://integratedbook.com/index1.html

- Instantpublisher.com
  P.O. Box 985, Collierville, TN 38027
  P) 800-259-2592 P) 901-853-7070 F) 901-853-6196
  www.instantpublisher.com
  questions@instantpublisher.com

- Keystone Digital Press
  210 Carter Drive, West Chester, PA 19382
  P) 610-344-9118
  www.kdpress.com
  sales@kdpress.com

- Kimco On Demand Printers
  4120 Brighton Blvd., Suite A-21, Denver, CO 80216
  P) 888-345-4626 F) 303-295-2754

- King Printing Company, Inc.
  181 Industrial Ave., East, Lowell, MA 01852
  www.kingprinting.com
  information@kingprinting.com

- Lake Book Manufacturing
  2085 North Cornell Avenue, Melrose Park, IL 60160
  P) 708-345-7000 F) 708-345-1544
  www.lakebook.com

- Lightning Source, Inc.
  1246 Heil Quaker Blvd,.La Vergne, TN 37086
  P) 615-213-5815 P) 615-213-4477 F) 615-213-4426
  www.lightningsource.com
  inquiry@lightningsource.com

- ➢ Malloy, Inc.
  5411 Jackson Road, Ann Arbor, MI 48103-1865
  P) 734-655-6113 P) 800-722-3231 F) 734-665-2326
  www.malloy.com

- ➢ Marrakech Express Inc.
  720 Wesley Ave, Tarpon Springs, FL 34689
  P) 800-940-6566 P) 813-942-2218 F) 813-937-4758
  print@marrak.com

- ➢ McNaughton & Gunn, Inc.
  960 Woodland Drive, P.O. Box 10, Saline, MI 48176
  P) 800-677-2665 P) 734-429-5411 F) 800-677-2665
  www.mcnaughton-gunn.com

- ➢ Media Lithographics, Inc.
  6080 Triangle Drive, City of Commerce, CA 90040
  P) 323-888-8997
  www.medialitho.com

- ➢ Medius Corporation
  1103 Montague Court, Milpitas, CA 94035
  P) 408-519-5000 P) 408-519-5049 F) 408-519-5002
  www.mediuscorp.com

- ➢ Mercury Print Productions
  50 Holleder Parkway, Rochester, NY 14615
  P) 585-458-7900 F) 585-458-2896
  www.mercuryprint.com
  mail@mercuryprint.com

- ➢ MOPC Inc.
  579 S. State College Blvd, Fullerton, CA 92831
  P) 714-871-5560 F) 714-871-5601

- Morgan Printing
  900 Old Koenig Lane #135, Austin, TX 78756
  P) 800-421-5593 P) 512-459-5194 F) 512-451-0755
  www.morganprinting.org
  mprinting@austin.rr.com

- Mosaic Press LLC
  3543 Indian Creek Road, Ste A, P.O. Box 436
  Happy Camp, CA 96039
  P) 530-493-2249
  mosaic@sisqtel.net

- Network Printers
  1010 S. 70th Street, Milwaukee, WI 53214
  P) 414-443-0530 F) 414-443-0536
  www.network-printers.com
  info@network-printers.com

- Odyssey Press Inc.
  22 Nadeau Drive, P.O. Box 7307, Gonic, NH 03839-7307
  P) 603-749-4433 F) 603-749-1425
  www.odysseypress.com
  opi@oddysseypress.com

- Offset Paperback Manufacturers
  P.O. Box N, Dallas, PA 18612
  P) 570-673-5261 F) 570-675-8714

- On-Demand Technologies, Inc.
  2220 Tomlynn Street, Richmond, VA 23230
  www.on-demandtech.com
  P) 804-359-4087 F) 804-359-4258

- Patterson Printing
  1550 Territorial Road, Benton Harbor, MI 49022
  P) 800-848-8826 F) 269-925-6057
  www.patterson-printing.com

- Phillips Brothers
  1555 W. Jefferson, P.O. Box 580, Springfield, IL 62705
  P) 800-637-9327 P) 217-787-3014 F) 217-787-9624
  www.pbpweb.com
  forinfo@pbpweb.com

- Phoenix Color
  540 Western Maryland Parkway, Hagerstown, MD 21740
  P) 800-632-4111
  www.phoenixcolor.com

- Pinnacle Press
  2662 Metro Blvd., St. Louis, MO 63043
  P) 800-760-0010 P) 314-291-2230 F) 314-291-8842
  www.pinnaclepress.com

- P.O.D. Wholesale
  519 W. Lancaster Avenue, Haverford, PA 19041
  P) 610-520-2500 F) 610-519-0261
  info@podwholesale.com
  www.podwholesale.com

- The Press of Ohio
  3765 Sunnybrook Rd., Brimfield, Ohio 44240
  P) 330-678-5868 F) 330-677-8256
  www.press-of-ohio.com

- Prime Mover
  9999 Muirlands Blvd., Irvine, CA 92618
  P) 949-251-8771
  www.primemover.net
  hugo@primemover.net

- Printing House
  540 Business Park Circle, Stoughton, WI 53589 USA
  P) 800-873-8990 P) 608-873-4500 F) 800-873-5910
  sales@printinghouseinc.com
  www.printinghouseinc.com

- Publishers' Graphics, LLC
  290 Gerzevske Lane, Carol Stream, IL 60188-2056
  P) 888-404-3769 P) 630-221-1850 F) 630-221-1870
  www.pubgraphics.com
  sales@pubgraphics.com

- Quinn Woodbine
  419 Park Avenue S., Ste. 1201
  New York, NY 10016
  P) 212-889-0552 F) 212-679-8156
  www.quinnwoodbine.com

- Robinson Graphics Inc.
  217 Connell Street, Goodlettsville, TN 37072
  P) 615-859-4875
  rginc@comcast.net

- Rose Printing Company Inc.
  2503 Jackson Bluff Road, Tallahassee, FL 32304
  P) 800-227-3725 P) 850-576-4151 F) 850-576-4153
  www.roseprinting.com

- R. R. Donnelley & Sons
  77 W. Wacker Drive, Chicago, IL 60601
  P) 312-326-8000
  www.rrdonnelley.com

- Sentinel Printing Company, Inc.
  250 Highway 10 North, St Cloud, MN 56304
  P) 800-450-6434 P) 320-251-6434 F) 320-251-6273
  www.sentinelprinting.com
  dhinman@sentinelprinting.com

- Sharp Offset Printing & Academy Books
  10 Cleveland Ave, P.O. Box 757, Rutland, Vermont 05701
  P) 800-356-3002 P) 802-773-9194 F) 802-773-6892
  www.sharpoffsetprinting.com
  info@sharpoffsetprinting.com

- ➤ Sheridan Books, Inc.
  P.O. Box 370, 613 E. Industrial Dr., Chelsea, MI 48118
  P) 800-999-BOOK P) 734-475-9145 F) 734-475-7337
  www.sheridanbooks.com

- ➤ Sheridan Printing
  1425 Third Avenue, Alpha, NJ 08865
  P) 908-454-0700 P) 908-213-8994 F) 908-454-2554
  www.sheridanprinting.com
  sheridanprint@entermail.net

- ➤ Signature Book Printing, Inc.
  8041 Cessna Avenue, Suite 132, Gaithersburg, MD 20879
  P) 301-258-8353 F) 301-670-4147
  www.signature-book.com
  book@sbpbooks.com

- ➤ Sterling Pierce
  422 Atlantic Avenue, East Rockaway, NY 11518
  P) 516-593-1170 F) 516-593-1401
  info@sterlingpierce.com
  www.sterlingpierce.com

- ➤ Stinehour Press
  853 Lancaster Road,Lunenburg, Vermont 05906
  P) 800-331-7753 P) 802-328-2507 F) 802-328-3960
  www.stinehourpress.com
  services@stinehourpress.com

- ➤ Technical Communication Services
  110 West 12th Ave., North Kansas City, MO 64116
  P) 816-842-9770 F) 816-842-0628
  www.tcsbook.com
  customerservice@tcsbook.com

- ➤ Thomson-Shore, Inc.
  7300 W. Joy Road, Dexter, Michigan 48130
  P) 734-426-3939 F) 800-706-4545 F) 734-426-6216

www.tshore.com

- Toppan Printing Co. of America
  1100 Randolph Rd., Somerset, NJ 08873
  P) 732-469-8400 F) 732-469-1868
  njsales@ta.toppan.com
  www.ta.toppan.com

- Total Printing Systems
  103 E. Morgan, Newton, IL 62448
  P) 800-465-5200 F) 618-783-8407
  www.tps1.com
  sales@tps1.com

- Trade Printing Services, LLC.
  2080 Las Palmas Drive, Carlsbad, CA 92009
  P) 760-496-0230 ext. 27 F) 760-496-0226
  www.tradeprintingsvc.com

- Trade Service Publications
  10996 Torreyana Road, San Diego, CA 92121
  P) 619-457-5920 P) 800-854-1527 F) 619-558-5989
  www.tradeservicepubs.com

- United Book Press
  1807 Whitehead Road, Baltimore, MD 21207
  P) 410-944-4044 P) 800-726-0120 F) 410-944-4049
  unitedbook@aol.com

- United Graphics Inc.
  1230 S. 57th Avenue, Cicero, IL 60804
  P) 708-780-7728 F) 708-780-7847
  www.bookmanufacturing.com

- Van Volumes, Ltd
  2 Springfield St, P.O. Box 314, Three Rivers, MA 01080
  P) 413-283-8556 P) 800-290-0462 F) 413-283-7884
  www.vanvolumes.com

vanvol@vanvolumes.com

➢ Vaughan Printing
411 Cowan Street, Nashville, TN 37207
P) 615-256-2244 F) 615-259-4576
www.vaughanprinting.com
sales@vaughanprinting.com

➢ Versa Press
1465 Spring Bay Rd, P.O. Box 2460, East Peoria, IL 61611
P) 800-447-7829 P) 309-822-8272 F) 309-822-8141
www.versapress.com
salessupport@versapress.com

➢ Victor Graphics
1211 Bernard Drive, Baltimore, MD 21223
P) 410-233-8300 F) 410-233-8304
www.victorgraphics.com

➢ Von Hoffmann Graphics
400 S. 14th Avenue, Eldridge, IA 52748
P) 319-285-4800 F) 319-285-5164
www.vonhoffmann.com

➢ WhitMar Electronic Press
4885 Ronson Court, Ste E, San Diego, CA 92111
P) 858-499-0050 F) 858-499-0060
www.whitmar.net
info@whitmar.net

➢ Wimmer Companies
4650 Shelby Air Dr, Memphis, TN 38118
P) 800-548-2537 P) 901-362-8900 F) 800-794-9806
www.wimmerco.com
wimmer@wimmerco.com

➢ Worzalla Printing
3535 Jefferson St., P.O. Box 307, Stevens Point, WI 54481
P) 715-344-9600 F) 715-344-2578
www.worzalla.com

MORE PUBLISHING BOOKS

A Basic Guide to Writing, Selling, and Promoting Children's Books: Plus Information about Self-Publishing
By Betsy B. Lee

ABCS of Self-Publishing: A Guide to Self-Publishing That Helps Ease the Way into Print
By Britt Bell

A Guide to Book Printing and Self-Publishing
By Gorham Printing

A Guide to Book Publishing
By Datus C. Smith, Jr.

For Black Writers: A Personal Account of How to Write, Publish & Market Your First Book
By Aliona L. Gibson

Get Published: Professionally, Affordably, Fast
By: Susan Driscoll and Diane Gedymin

Getting Published
By Sheree Bykofsky and Jennifer Basye Sander

Guerilla Marketing for Writers
By Jay Conrad Levinson, Rick Frishman & Michael Larsen

How to Get Published Free
By David Rising

How to Make Money from Home: Everything You Need to Know to Successfully Publish
By Lisa Shaw

How to Publish, Promote and Sell Your Own Book
By Robert Lawrence Holt

How to Publish and Promote Online
By M.J. Rose & Angela Adair Hey

How to Publish Your Own Book: Everything You Need to Know about the Self-Publishing Process
By Anna Crosbie

How to Self-Publish for Profit
By JaWar – **gojawar.com**

How to Self-Publish Your Book with Little or No Money! A complete Guide to Self-Publishing at a Profit
By Bettie E. Tucker and Wayne Brumagin

How to Start & Run a Small Book Publishing Company
By Peter I. Hupalo

How to Succeed in the Publishing Game
By Vickie M. Stringer

How to Write and Publish Your Own Book
Cuttie W. Bacon, III Ph.D Co-Author Cuttie W. Bacon, IV, MBA

Make Money Self-Publishing: Learn How from Fourteen Successful Small Publishers
By Suzanne P. Thomas

Print on Demand Book Publishing
By Morris Rosenthal

Publishing Gems: Insider Information for the Self-Publishing Writer
By Brent Sampson

Putting Your Passion Into Print
By Arielle Eckstut & David Henry Sterry

Self-Publishing 101
By Debbie Elicksen

Self-Publishing for Dummies
By Jason R. Rich

Self-Publishing Simplified
By Outskirtpress

Self-Publishing, Writing and Marketing Your Own Books and Booklets
By Cathy Pedigo

Smart Self-Publishing: An Author's Guide to Producing a Marketable Book
By Linda G. Salisbury and Jim Salisbury

So, You Want to Write a Cookbook
By Judy Rehmel

Start Your Own Self-Publishing Business
By Entrepreneur Press

The African-American Writer's Guide to Successful Self-Publishing
By Takesha D. Powell

The Clearly Confusing World of Self-Publishing and POD
By Clea Saal

The Complete Guide to Self-Publishing
By Tom & Marilyn Ross

The Complete Idiot's Guide to Publishing Children's Books
By Harold D. Underdown

The Complete Self-Publishing Handbook: A Step-by-step Guide to Producing and Marketing Your Own Book

By David M. Brownstone & Irene M. Franck

The Copyright Handbook: What Every Writer Needs to Know
By Attorney Stephen Fishman

The Fine Print of Self-Publishing
By Mark Levine

The Law in Plain English For Writers
By Leonard D. DuBoff & Bert P. Krages II Attorneys at Law

The Well-Fed Self-Publisher: How to Turn One Book into a Full Time Living (Well-Fed)
By Peter Bowerman

Official Contacts to Self-Publishing & Marketing
By James Hickman

The Self-Publishing Manual-How to Write, Print and Sell Your Own Book
By Dan Poynter

The Young Author's Do-It-Yourself Book: How to Write, Illustrate and Produce Your Own Book
By Donna Guthrie, Nancy Bentley and Katy Keck Arnsteen

Write a Book in 53 Days: How to Produce, Publish and Sell a Great Book During a Vacation
By Don Paul

JAWAR'S AUDIO BOOKS

Getting Book Distribution
Ten Ways to Make Money from Your Book
What You Didn't Know You to Ask About Self-Publishing?
What You Need to Know about Self-Publishing?

CREATING WEALTH

Whether you earn an additional $5,000 or $5,000,000 a year from your book publishing endeavors, remember to always put a percentage of your earnings (money that you make) aside, preferably in a tax-sheltered account and invest your money in businesses that have nothing to do with the book publishing industry. This is called "diversification of your assets (money)". In addition, you want to always pay yourself first, spend less money than you earn, carry little to no debt and keep accurate and complete records of the money you earn and spend. This will increase your chances for long-term wealth creation and retention. Educate yourself about business and money; after all if you don't mind your business and money, someone else will. To ensure you advance your own learning on saving, investing and creating wealth I have listed a few terms below that you should know.

401(k)
Annuities
Assets
Asset Allocation
Bonds
- Corporate
- Convertible
- Government
CD-Certificate Deposit
Checking Account
Compounding Interest
Debt to Income Ratio
Diversification
Dollar-Cost Averaging
Earnings
Equity
Financial Freedom

Index Funds
Inflation
Investment Portfolio
IRA-Individual Retirement Account
Keoghs
Market Index
Money-Market Accounts
Money Market Mutual Funds
NAV (Net Asset Value)
No-Load Mutual Funds
Passive Income
Prospectus
Real Estate
Residual Income

ROI (Return on Investment)	Savings Account
ROI (Return on Investment)	**Savings Account**
Roth-IRA, SEP-IRA, Simple-IRA	**Stocks**
	Tax Sheltered Accounts
	Treasury Bills

Educate yourself about investing and seek the advice of professionals who may help you verify your information. Publications that may help you become familiar with saving and investing your money are Black Enterprise, The Wall Street Journal, Kiplinger, Money, Smart Money, Barron's, Investor Business Daily, Financial Times, the Business Section of the Atlanta Journal Constitution and the Money Section of USA Today. You will also want to read books such as Black & Green, Think & Grow Rich, Rich Dad Poor Dad and the Richest Man in Babylon. For more information on saving, investing and making your money grow; visit the following websites.

www.bankrate.com	**www.mfea.com**
www.blackenterprise.com	**www.money.com**
www.buyandhold.com	**www.moneyopolis.org**
www.creditinfocenter.com	**www.moringstar.com**
www.fool.com	**www.rothira.com**
www.indexfunds.com	**www.smartmoney.com**
www.investoreducation.org	**www.tiaacref.com**
www.jumpstartcoalition.org	**www.troweprice.com**
www.kiplinger.com	**www.youdecide.com**
www.marketwatch.com	**www.vanguard.com**

makemoneyselfpublishing.com

moneyonline.blogspot.com

moneygoldmine.blogspot.com

selfpublishforprofit.blogspot.com

DESIGN APART

**www
designapartstudio
com**

studio
404_351+4312

email
ashil@designapartstudio.com

Entertainment Business Support
ATLANTA • GA

Ph. 404.217.0696
email. kfennell@entertainmentbizsupport.com
web. www.entertainmentbizsupport.com

Make Money Online

Visit

makemoneyselfpublishing.com

moneygoldmine.blogspot.com

moneyonline.blogspot.com

gojawar.com

JAWAR

Chief Visionary Officer of Music Therapy 101, a Music Business Conference and Workshop Series since 1998, has given informative seminars in Atlanta-Georgia, Los Angeles-California, Washington D.C., Charlotte-North Carolina and Louisville-Kentucky. He created the workshop to identify and share vital information in a step-by-step process necessary for success and ultimate longevity in the music biz for aspiring artists and those willing to be involved in the music industry.

In 2002, JaWar created the MIC (Music Industry Connection) one of the few free all Music Business Publications that serves all genres of music. In just over a year, the MIC tripled its' circulation, doubled its' page count and increased its' subscription base. In 2004 JaWar expanded his publishing efforts and released the *Atlanta Music Industry Connection: Resources for Artists, Producers & Managers Book*, the most comprehensive directory of Atlanta Music Business Professionals in print. When your event demands practical, relevant, and useful details from an enthusiastic speaker who has legitimately "been there" by releasing the Dark Ages II & Paranormal Activity CDs on his independent record company Kemetic Records consider JaWar; he may be contacted at 800-963-0949, **gojawar.com** or P.O. Box 52682, Atlanta, GA 30355, USA.

JaWar provides music business consulting services, with an emphasis on marketing & promotions, strategic planning and increasing profit, to select businesses and individuals seeking to advance their companies goals and objectives. Whether through one-on-one consultation or in a business group setting, JaWar may help your business become more efficient and effective.

171

MAIL ORDER FORM

Please mail me the following music business items to help me achieve my goals. I have completed the attached order form and will include a money order for my total and mail it payable to:

MUSIC INDUSTRY CONNECTION, LLC
P.O. BOX 52682, Atlanta, GA 30355, USA

Name:	
Company Name:	
Mailing address:	
City:	State: Zip:
Phone:	Fax:
Email:	
Comments:	

www.gojawar.com 800-963-0949

Item Description	PRICE Per Item	# of Items	Total
How To Self-Publish for Profit Resources for Writers, Authors, Publishers	$19.95		
Atlanta Music Industry Connection Book: Resources for-Artists, Producers, Managers	$19.95		
Atlanta Modeling Industry: Secrets Revealed	$19.95		
MY Music MY Business	$19.95		
Los Angeles Music Industry Connection: Resources for-Artists, Producers, Managers	$19.95		
Music Industry Connection: The Truth About Record Pools & Music Conferences, Talent Shows & Open-Mics	$19.95		
18 FAQ's (Frequently Asked Questions) about the Music Biz by JaWar – **AUDIO BOOK**	$ 9.95		
SUBTOTAL	/////////		
Shipping & Handling Add $6.00			
GA residents add 7% sales tax.			
TOTAL			

www.ingramcontent.com/pod-product-compliance
Lightning Source LLC
Chambersburg PA
CBHW070802100426
42742CB00012B/2221